F

R. Gary Patterson

A FIRESIDE

BOOK

PUBLISHED

BY

SIMON &

SCHUSTER

THE
WAS PAUL

THE GREAT
BEATLE
DEATH
CLUES

FIRESIDE
Rockefeller Center
1230 Avenue of the Americas
New York, NY 10020

Copyright © 1996, 1998 by R. Gary Patterson

FIRESIDE and colophon are registered
trademarks of Simon & Schuster Inc.

Designed by Judy Wong

Manufactured in the United States of America

7   8   9   10

Library of Congress Cataloging-in-Publication Data
Patterson, R. Gary.
The walrus was Paul : the great Beatle death clues /
R. Gary Patterson.
p.   cm.
Includes bibliographical references and index.
1. McCartney, Paul.   2. Rock musicians—England—Biography.
3. Beatles.   I. Title.
[ML410.M115P42   1998]
782.42166'092'2—dc21   98-34607
CIP
MN
ISBN 0-684-85062-1 (pbk.)

For Shea ...

CONTENTS

CONTENTS

FOREWORD

Perhaps you own every conceivable item of Beatles' memorabilia available. Perhaps you own every record, 45 rpm or album, or CD ever recorded by the Beatles. A bootleg disc might possibly be in your collection as well. The intangible magic that came with owning a Beatles' record came not only in the music, but in viewing the artwork on the album cover. That picture that fronted the latest Beatles' record. When it was released, you rushed to the store to get the latest Beatles' masterpiece. As you sat next to your record player listening with such overwhelming intensity, you kept your hands and eyes busy as well by looking at every square inch of that album cover, over and over again. You memorized it. You could describe that cover, as well as the music, in your sleep.

Imagine, if you will, being within the storm of Beatlemania. To actually be one of those talented four musicians. Unfortunately, they had very little freedom. How did they entertain *themselves* during those quiet moments?

Creativity flowed like a boiling river within the Beatles. We heard it in their music that, even to this day, high school and college literature classes interpret. Within this hurricane of creativity came an idea; an idea that I still believe was the greatest hoax ever pulled off. A simple "who done it" was instilled in the music of the greatest band in the world. The idea was Paul McCartney was killed in a car accident and an imposter was filling in within the Beatles.

Oh, the Beatles could have gone public and said, "By the way. Paul is dead and this is someone else sitting in for him." Where is the fun in that statement? What would truly be adventurous would be to put in little clues throughout the music, and on that incredible album cover artwork. Ah yes, little clues that when all put together would actually tell the gruesome nightmarish story of the decapitation of Paul McCartney. And, then, to add mystery to the story . . . Whenever anyone asked, respond with total ignorance.

I remember hearing this most interesting and peculiar story in 1969. I was in the seventh grade in Virginia Beach, Virginia, listening to WNOR-FM. The news came of this strange finding and they began airing the clues. I sat, with incredible focus for that age, and began piecing the story together. When they aired "Revolution 9" backwards, I remember, the room got cold! I'm sure it was my own body temperature changing from all the excitement, but I swear the room got cold! I shivered at the sounds that were coming over *my* radio! From my favorite band! I couldn't believe what I was hearing. Could this actually be true? It was too bizarre but it was there—*I could hear it!*

Five years later, when I began a career of my own in radio, I begged for the opportunity to explain the strange story to other Beatles' fans. It wasn't until 1993, when I finally made it to the ABC Radio Network, that I got my chance to lay it all out on the air for the listeners. I was given what I consider my dream handed to me on a platter . . . I had a radio show playing oldies with a spotlight on the Beatles . . . *Beatle Archives!* Just as if it were a clue within a Beatles' song or on their album cover, coincidence I suppose, R. Gary Patterson and I made a connection. I had heard of his book, *The Walrus Was Paul: The Great Beatle Death Clues,* and I immediately contacted him on the phone. I told him of my Beatles' show, and how I wanted to reconstruct all the clues for my Halloween edition of *Beatle Archives.* He and I made an incredible connection. The chemistry was perfect. I knew he had the same passion for this topic as I did. He joined me via phone and together we produced a radio show that caused an unbelievable reaction from listeners! I was truly surprised at how many people had never heard of this hoax. The calls kept coming, begging me to re-air the special. The next year I devoted two shows to this topic, and still the phone calls came. I found that once you hear the clues being laid out before you, it becomes impossible to deny that the Fab Four had something up their sleeves. Then, on Thanksgiving Day 1995, Paul McCartney telephoned the network from his studio in London to thank America for its support for *Anthology 1.* It was during this conversation that, finally, something was admitted concerning the death clues. When talking about the "Free as a Bird" video, with all its references to other Beatles' songs, he stated, "We used to make a game of putting little clues in all our music back then. . . ." I couldn't contain myself. I grabbed the phone and called Gary Patterson that very moment to let him know I had it on tape! Paul McCartney admitted it!

It is also interesting to watch how others have picked up on the clues heard on *Beatle Archives* and have taken them onto the Internet. During the second radio special devoted to this topic, Gary and I unveiled a *new* clue, within the lyrics of "Blue Jay

Way." When reversed, George Harrison's lyrics "Please don't be long . . ." turns into "Paul is bloody, Paul is very, very bloody." It didn't take long to realize that Gary was onto something new and just as interesting as all previous clues. The world jumped to respond with agreement. Way to go, Gary!

Having lived through the entire "Paul is dead" era, and now having the opportunity to relive that golden mystery once again, is without a doubt one of the highlights of my career.

Everyone who remembers this time or anyone who has never heard of this incredible hoax owes it to themselves to sit down and carefully savor every word of this book! Even non-Beatles' fans will enjoy this mystery tour through the greatest hoax ever.

You'll never listen to a Beatles' record the same way again. Actually, now you'll finally hear the Beatles' music!

—Jay Fox
ABC Radio Network

ACKNOWLEDGMENTS

 I would like to acknowledge several works that greatly helped me in my research. First of all, William Dowlding's *Beatle Songs* was a vast resource of material collected from various Beatle interviews and saved me many hours of research. Also, Dowlding listed a series of death clues found in his research.

David Sheff's fascinating *Playboy Interviews with John Lennon and Yoko Ono* provided Lennon's remembrances of the development of each Lennon and McCartney composition. I would also like to mention each of the following highly recommended works that served as inspiration: Peter Brown and Steven Gaines' *The Love You Make: An Insiders' Story of the Beatles;* Tom Schultheiss' *A Day in the Life: The Beatles Day-By-Day, 1960–1970;* Chris Salewicz's *McCartney;* Philip Norman's *Shout! The Beatles in Their Own Generation;* Derek Taylor's *It Was Twenty Years Ago Today: The Story of Sgt. Pepper's Lonely Hearts Club Band;* Barbara Suczek's *The Curious Case of the*

Death of Paul McCartney; and John Neary's "The Magical Mc-Cartney Mystery" for *Life* magazine.

I would also like to thank these individuals for their help and inspiration: Shea (my beautiful daughter, who often complained of being born too late and missing the Beatles, Woodstock, and the excitement of the sixties); Mark Hightower, guardian of the sacred Beatles' relics, without whose help this effort would not have been possible; Dan Lane, my editor at Fireside Books whose encouragement and vision has made this possible; Mark Ryan and Eric Alterman, my agents who work long and hard hours for me; Norman Gillis, my attorney; Wally Saukerson and *Wally World*; Maryglenn Jordan and Dowling Press, Inc.; Mark, Myra, and John at JM Productions; Mark Lapidos and *Beatlefest;* Charles Rosenay!!! and David Schwartz of *Good Day Sunshine* (the world's number-one Beatle fanzine); Bill King and *Beatlefan* magazine; Ramona Simmons; Ben Blanton; David and Varilyn Smith; Jason; Howie and *The Music Machine* in Baltimore; Mark Hughes; Chet Bobin (the number-one Beatles' fan from Texas); Jay Nations; Ken Goans; Glenn Neuwirth and "Sea of Timeless Records"; Tom; Mike and Maria Armstrong and "Lost and Found Records"; Craig Hampel; Walt Adams of TNN; Daisey V. Dunlap; Ted Hall and Kim Stephens of WBIR-TV (Knoxville); Natalie Dick and Russ Murphy of WATE-TV (Knoxville); Wayne Bledsoe of *The Knoxville News Sentinel;* Delores (my wonderful wife, muse, and partner, without whom this would not have been possible); Denny and my incredible mother, Ruby M. Hunt (who showed me nothing but unconditional love and unquestioned support); as well as everyone else in my whole family, who was always there for me and gave me much more than I can ever return. A very special thanks to Kanya Mullins for her help and dedication to this project. This book is written in loving memory of "Two Mamas and Pop," and my father, Rudolph G. Patterson.

I would also like to thank the following radio personalities for their support—without a doubt they are the best in the business: Jim Zippo and J. Fox "The Fox That Rocks" from the ABC Radio Network; Cam Gardiner CKLW (Ontario, Canada); Jeff McKee, Richmond's XL-102; Lou and Larry of Des Moines' 95-KGGO; Simon and the BBC; Tim and Mark from Phoenix's 93.3 KDKB (the best Beatles' fans anywhere and the best on-air interviews!); Joe Johnson's *Beatle Brunch,* and *Radio Caroline* in New Zealand. I would also like to thank *Beatle Archives* (Jay Fox and ABC Radio) and *The Beatle Years* both, along with *Beatle Brunch,* the best syndicated radio shows for Beatles' fans anywhere.

I would like to say thank you to a growing number of young Beatles' fans who continue to keep the faith and the Beatles' music alive. It has been an honor to give interviews, as well as form many new friendships, with a number of teenage fans who compose informative biweekly Beatles' newsletters and create brilliant web sites dedicated to the timeless music of the Fab Four. One day,while I was online, I received an instant message from a SgtPep7784. This young Beatles' fan from New York opened my eyes to the thousands of young Beatles' fans who have developed amazing web pages and are truly experts in Beatles' history and trivia. I would like to thank you, Jen, for allowing me to see firsthand how the Beatles' legacy is being kept alive for a new generation. I highly recommend Dan Phillips' "Sgt. Pepper's Lonely Hearts Club Band Online," as well as Dustin Tittle's "Beatle Forum" as excellent sites for Beatles' information. The newsletters are excellent and very well written. When it comes to the "Paul is dead" rumors, one of the more interesting sites is maintained by Daniel Parker, kalamazoo7.

These young writers may well be the next generation of writers for *Good Day Sunshine* and *Beatlefan*. I would also like to thank the many fans who are so supportive and continuously suggest more and more clues.

In closing, I have to say that while online one afternoon I received a strange e-mail request. It was signed, simply, Tom. As I corresponded with Tom he told me about a call he made to a certain radio show in Detroit, Michigan, on the night of October 12, 1969. Tom had now found me. So, I will let Tom have the last word and set up the introduction for one of the strangest chapters in rock-and-roll history.

"I am sure Nostradamus' writings must have gotten dismissed and ignored to be lost and forgotten until another age. Likewise, this 'Is he really dead?' myth that the media pumped out (something much different) gave publicity or credence to 'the clues.' So much was made of this that the *Abbey Road* album (which was considered a 'dud') started to sell again.

"I believe that it came out just one month-and-a-half before. Our campus bookstore had already dismantled the display for it and put it away. Then the sales really took off. Since Beatles' music was played nationwide from coast to coast the day of my call—because they believed that Paul McCartney had died, stations would give one of the greatest albums ever made air play. And all Beatle records had to be re-released, due to the demand. Many of the vinyl records were worn out from being played—unfortunately—in *both* directions. If anything, Paul had been rescued from obscurity."

Tom, when did you first hear the clues?

"I first heard the rumors about the clues from friends on a college campus in Ypsilanti, Michigan, just west of Detroit, near Ann Arbor. Someone from Illinois on campus later sought me out. He may have been a source for some of the clues. It seems to validate some of the other Illinois connections that I have read about. But, I worked as long and hard on this much the way you did, Gary, or that the kids that I see nowadays do putting together web sites. Hardly slept back then, it seemed. Roommates claim that they never saw me work so hard. So many of the clues I put together myself."

Tell me about the call to the Gibb Show.

"I spent two hours live on the air on the WKNR call-in line reciting the clues, and telling Russ how to cue the records up to the right spot to hear 'I buried Paul' or 'Turn me on, dead man.' He played records and, in between, I was on the air with him. He was skeptical, but he stayed with me because he was so caught up with interest. He had never heard of any of this before. It took about all of that time though, and I was real tired when it was over.

"Then I visited the station, about an hour later, with two friends along for the fun. By then McCartney himself had already called WKNR from Scotland, in quite a state of rage, I hear, trying to put a stop to the story. I met Uncle Russ (Gibb), and he interviewed me live in the station, and his show concluded its air slot, without resolving the matter. I tried to explain that this wasn't a serious thing as him being really dead, but that didn't seem to matter. The media had run away with the story."

What has happened to you since the Gibb show?

"Only about a dozen people came up to me at school telling me about how they heard me on the air, or that someone told them about it. A TV special on Detroit PBS was made with

Russ and F. Lee Bailey (who manually reached over himself and clicked on the tape playing my voice).

"Everyone that I knew had been wrapped up with the clues for so very long. Then campus life went on just as before for me. Attempts to get into radio DJ work introduced me to the reality of life, in that there wasn't much chance of earning a good living at such a job for me. I had to get a haircut and 'get a real job!' Without the distinction of the mystery taking up my time, I never paid any mind to what I had done—for twenty-five years!

"While alone watching VJ Adam Curry announce on MTV that it had been 'Twenty-five years since the Paul-is-dead hoax' and 'Who would want to start such a rumor and why?' This put chills up my back. Had it really been twenty-five years? Am I that old already? Peter Pan was never going to grow up . . . and neither was I. Now the reality of the passage of time hit me like a rock!

"About four years ago, the Detroit papers re-covered the story when McCartney toured the city. Mom sent the article to me by mail. I told the story over the phone to my brother-in-law, although he didn't really seem to take it in as though he believed all of what I claimed. Then, he left a message one night with my wife that he had heard CNN carry a story. He had heard in the piece 'my voice' from a station log recording asking if Russ Gibb had ever heard the clues, and claiming it was started by someone named 'Tom.'

"So few people knew that I was that fellow. But so many folks follow the clues. I have, after twenty-eight years, recently surfed the Internet's search engines and found that I am . . . well, like famous. It's my fifteen minutes."

Tom, what message should today's generation get from this?

"They should know their history well enough to learn from it. Growing up means putting meaning behind the sayings of sages like:

"'Love is all you need.'

"'She says she loves you, and you know you should be glad.'

"'Living is easy with eyes closed.'

"'Strawberry Fields Forever' (nonpoetic translation: 'Don't worry, be happy')

"'Don't believe everything you hear, and half of what you read.'

"'In the future, everyone will be famous for fifteen minutes.'

"'Oh, and 'Rumors of my death have been greatly exaggerated.'"

Thanks, Tom!

*In memory of
my dad, Gentry D. Hunt:
Fathers are determined by
much more than chromosomes.
Instead, fathers are determined
by their many unselfish acts
of unconditional love.*

INTRODUCTION

 In order to develop a better understanding of the significance of the "Paul is dead" rumors, the reader should consider each clue as fitting into one of three major categories:

1. **The totally ridiculous:** Some of these clues fit into the mystery as gently as a sledgehammer splintering a round peg into a square hole. A number of these clues are rumor or hearsay and cannot be confirmed, but many of them are hilarious. I'll leave these for you to decipher. It is, after all, a mystery tour . . . right?

2. **Guided looking and guided listening:** Warning! Clues in this category can be the things nightmares are made of. Once you see the clues or hear the hidden messages in a reversed tape you will never forget it. Pleasant dreams!

3. **The unexplained:** These clues had to be placed by the Beatles themselves. For what purpose, we may never know! Perhaps you can take up the quest and, with this book as your guide, solve this incredible puzzle of Beatlemania.

PROLOGUE

 December 8, 1980, was a typical winter's night in East Tennessee. I had just taken my car to a small minimart in Oak Ridge to fill it with gasoline. My English literature students were struggling with Shakespeare's *Macbeth* and my radio was, as always, blasting out the rock sounds of WIMZ radio. Then, an emergency announcement came over the airwaves. In a frantic voice, the late night DJ announced that John Lennon had been shot and killed by an assassin. It was approximately 11:45 P.M.. That tragic news reawakened a fear that I had felt only once before, back in 1963.

On November 22, 1963, I was in my eighth-grade classroom awaiting a scheduled visit to the friendly dentist, when the school intercom interrupted my daydreams of hypodermic needles and novocaine with a stunning announcement: President John F. Kennedy had been shot in Dallas, and was presumed dead. President Kennedy's death made me question my future, at the tender age of thirteen. Where were we going? What would be our fate?

Sixteen years later, the death of John Lennon prompted the same fearful questions, but had a more profound effect upon my consciousness than the Kennedy assassination. While Kennedy's death nearly shattered my hope for the future, John Lennon's death signaled the end of my youth.

I thought back to the night of February 9, 1964, when I first watched the Beatles perform on *The Ed Sullivan Show.* Like millions of others, I was swept away by the band's overpowering charisma. I immediately rushed out and bought "I Want to Hold Your Hand"—an act I would repeat countless times in the coming years. A moptop haircut soon followed, even though my high school adhered to a strict dress code, including a rule that boys' hair could not touch their eyebrows, ears, or shirt collars. I began playing the guitar and practiced until my hands were numb. As those memories passed through my mind once again, I realized that the idealism of my youth had become exactly that: a memory.

The next day, at Oliver Springs High School, I prepared a memorial for John Lennon. My students and I played Beatles' records and interpreted their lyrics. We spoke of the importance of youth and how each of us should set goals and strive to fulfill those goals. I explained how each of us should charge into life and make it count for something. What I couldn't begin to explain was why Lennon's senseless killing had come to pass.

I had always hoped the Beatles would get back together for one more concert. Of course, this was a selfish desire, a longing for one more taste of my carefree youth. A female fan, probably having the same thoughts as I, once asked Lennon the question, "When are the Beatles getting back together again?" to which he replied, "When are you going back to high school?"

Lennon's Socratic answer made the point simply and perfectly: We can never go home again. The secret of life is to go forward and keep growing, to forgive your own mistakes, and search for complete happiness.

Thank you, John, Paul, George, and Ringo for the pleasure you brought me and countless other fans.

CHAPTER I

I
Buried
Paul

THE
BRITISH
INVASION
AND THE
AMERICAN
MASS
MEDIA

The Beatles were the musical messiahs of the turbulent sixties. John Lennon, Paul McCartney, George Harrison, and Ringo Starr led the British invasion that overran America's youth. No other British force, from Henry Clinton and George Cornwallis to Sir Edward Pakenham, accomplished so convincing a victory upon American soil. The method of conquest was not with fire and sword, but with electric guitars, amplifiers, and fab songs that infected every American household with the Mersey Beat.

American television, that unsuspecting British ally, innocently brought the Beatles into our living rooms on February 9, 1964, mainly due to the foresight of Ed Sullivan. But not even Sullivan, the promoter who introduced the American public to the likes of Robert Goulet and Elvis, foresaw the tidal wave that was about to hit American shores.

On that peaceful winter night, the home-viewing audience was said to have numbered well over seventy-three million

Americans. Although a veteran of the television wars, Ed Sullivan must have been amazed that this British group was such a huge draw. Elvis Presley had set the record for the highest number of studio tickets requested: over seven thousand for his appearance in 1958. In what was a foreshadowing of things to come, the show had received over sixty thousand requests for tickets to the Beatle performance (Schaffner, 14). Though some sources maintain that the television studio's seating capacity was only seven hundred, eight hundred tickets were given out through an impartial drawing, and those breathless individuals, chosen by fate, became live witnesses to the surrender of American youth.

The Beatles' form of rock and roll blazed like wildfire through record stores and television dance shows (*American Bandstand; Ready, Steady, Go!; Hullabaloo;* and *Shindig*). A new culture and art form, one that America sorely needed, was born.

The Beatles' moptop haircuts, Nehru jackets, and Cuban-heeled boots, not to mention their tight harmonies and melodies, helped combat the grief of a country still reeling from the untimely assassination of John F. Kennedy—the president who, more than any other, symbolized an era of youth, hope, and opportunity.

Unfortunately, rock and roll proved to be just as susceptible to the same tragedies that seemed to infuse so many other aspects of American life during the sixties. On February 3, 1959, just a few miles outside Clear Lake, Iowa, Buddy Holly, Ritchie Valens, and the Big Bopper perished in a fiery plane crash. The next year, Eddie Cochran died of injuries received in an automobile accident on April 17, 1960. Holly, Valens, the Big Bopper, and Cochran had all died tragically at the very height of their fame. On October 12, 1969 radio call-in lines across the country were backlogged with urgent requests from hysterical fans who demanded an answer to the same question: Had Beatle Paul McCartney died, too?

On October 12, 1969, Russ Gibb, disk jockey for Detroit's underground station WKNR-FM, received the phone call that would launch an unprecedented outbreak of hysteria throughout the pop world. The caller, who gave his name only as Tom, suggested that Gibb listen carefully to the fadeouts of certain Beatle songs. The Beatles' *Abbey Road* had just been released, but this early investigation concentrated on "Revolution 9" from *The Beatles* (the White Album) as well as the muffled murmuring at the conclusion of "Strawberry Fields Forever." As Gibb listened intently, he heard what seemed to be a number of references that seemed to suggest that Paul McCartney had met with an untimely end (Schaffner, 129).

Many claim that one of the first written reports of the "Paul is dead" rumor was an article written by Tim Harper that appeared in a college newspaper in Des Moines, Iowa, on September 17, 1969. The article, "Is Paul Dead?" also appeared in the *Chicago Sun-Times* on October 21, 1969 (Hockinson, 97). WABC-AM (New York City) DJ Robey Younge also remembered receiving mysterious calls from some of his listeners begging him to help get the tragic story to the outside world. WABC-AM was a powerful station, especially at night, and could sometimes reach forty states with its broadcast signal. In an exclusive interview with my friend Joe Johnson for his syndicated *Beatle Brunch* radio program, Younge recounted his role in the McCartney mystery. 'Paul McCartney dead' is something I did one strange night after some kids had called me up from the Midwest, 'cause I was on the late night show and the signal went all across the country. They said this, that, and the other. They said, 'Here are the clues,' and I laughed at them. I went on the air that night and I laughed at them. I said, 'This is ridiculous.' That night I went home and couldn't sleep. I couldn't get any rest. I thought, 'What are these kids talking about? What clues?' So, I went to my record cabinet and I started playing these records backwards as they had instructed me to and, sure enough, there emerged some very strange stuff. . . . It was a big game in those days to uncover the clues. The kids told me, 'We hear you coming through loud and clear, why don't you blow the whistle on this?' So, I did. Oddly enough, on that same night somebody at *The Tonight Show* taping blurted from the audience, 'Paul is dead.' I was the first one to broadcast it to a lot of people. The switchboard at WABC was jammed. The program director came down in the middle of the night in his pajamas with an armed guard saying, 'Robey, you're creating a national panic! Get off the air!' I said, 'Fine! Fine! It's all right with me.' I said, 'By the way, this is going to be one heck of a station promotion for Halloween.'"

Not to be outdone, Alex Bennett of radio station WMCA-AM in New York City added fuel to this macabre rumor. He followed the trail of clues to London, in order to unearth more facts. Bennett was so involved in his pursuit that he stated, "The only way McCartney is going to quell the rumors is by coming up with a set of fingerprints from a 1965 passport which can be compared to his present prints." Bennett presented the so-called evidence to the public through his call-in radio show.

A whole cast of characters became involved in the search for death clues, as the wave of hysteria reached ever greater heights. Incredibly, there was a television special in which F. Lee Bailey questioned a number of witnesses, including Beatles' manager Allen Klein, and Peter Asher, the brother of Jane Asher, Paul McCartney's one-time fiancee, and member of the rock group Peter and Gordon. As Klein and Asher denied any and all evidence supporting the conclusion that Paul McCartney had met with a tragic demise, Gibb and fellow investigators took an active role in the telecast, and presented the grim evidence to the viewing public. At times Klein and Asher seemed bewildered as they tried to give a proper explanation for the preponderance of evidence gathered by Gibb, Fred Labour, and the other sleuths. The special ended with Bailey's suggestion that the public make up its own mind about the facts. Interestingly enough, no video copy of this television special remains. No one seems to remember what happened to the master tapes!

The evidence revolved around the theory that Paul McCartney had been decapitated in an automobile wreck after he left Abbey Road studios, apparently upset over an argument with the other Beatles. McCartney took a ride in his Aston Martin sports car and perished horribly in the ensuing accident. This accident supposedly took place in November 1966, most probably on a Tuesday (Schaffner, 127). One version of the tragic accident has a despondent Paul picking up a female hitch-hiker, who later unknowingly caused the accident by her over-enthusiasm to get closer to the pop icon. The mystery girl's name was supposedly Rita, since in the song "Lovely Rita" from the *Sgt. Pepper's Lonely Hearts Club Band* album McCartney sings, "I took her home. I nearly made it." Many listeners were convinced that this was another reference to the car crash.

According to William J. Dowlding's *Beatle Songs*, "McCartney did have a car crash on a Wednesday at 5 A.M.. It happened on November 9, 1966, after an all-night recording session, and was coincidentally the morning after John met Yoko" (Dowlding, 158). As his sources, Dowlding cited H. V. Fulpen's *The Beatles: An Illustrated Diary*, and *The Macs: Mike McCartney's Family Album*, written by Michael McCartney, Paul's brother.

According to Michael McCartney, Paul had a crash on a motor-bike that caused "severe facial injuries to one half of his baby face" (Dowlding, 158).

In *McCartney*, Chris Salewicz gives the following descrip-tion of the accident. It appears that sometime late in 1966 Paul was in Liverpool to spend a few days with his father. While there, Paul and Tara Browne, the Guinness heir, who was al-ready at the McCartney home as a guest of Paul's brother Mike McCartney, had smoked a joint together one quiet evening and had then decided to ride a pair of mopeds to visit Paul's Aunt Bett. (Paul's stepsister, Ruth McCartney, claims that Paul and Browne had stopped at a nearby pub and had a few too many drinks.) Shortly before arriving at Aunt Bett's house, Paul lost control of his motorbike and was thrown across the handlebars into the street. McCartney landed on his face and received a nasty cut on his upper lip. Since this was just no accident vic-tim, but a Beatle, the McCartney family realized that a private doctor would have to be called. This would avoid the mass of Beatlemania that would surely overwhelm the hospital. The doctor arrived at Aunt Bett's home, and stitched up the wound. A few months later, Paul was said to have grown his heavy mus-tache for *Sgt. Pepper's* cover to conceal the scar until it healed properly. It appeared that Paul also suffered a chipped tooth in the accident. In the "Paperback Writer" and "Rain" videos Paul appears to have a missing tooth. Of course, this gave yet more evidence to the great imposter theory, as did the noticeable scar that can be seen over Paul's upper lip in his individual photo from the White Album, released in 1968.

The biggest problem with the theory that Paul's death re-sulted from an automobile accident, not the simple motorbike crash, was the absence of any concrete evidence. Surely there were records—a death certificate or autopsy report—that could substantiate this bizarre occurrence. Another unanswered question dealt with the lack of eyewitnesses. Such an extraordinary occurrence would have proved very lucrative for any opportunistic spectator willing to cash in on his or her knowledge of the disastrous event. One unfounded rumor suggested that the charred remains of a young man had been found following a car crash. He was said to have received severe head injures, and that proper police identification was impossible due to the cadaver's missing teeth. Of course, there is no record of such an accident at that time, but this is yet one more clue to the ultimate urban legend of rock and roll.

On October 14, 1969, two days after the rumor broke on WKNR-FM, the *Michigan Daily* ran a review of the latest Beatles' album, *Abbey Road*. The review, written by Fred LaBour, took the form of an obituary, illustrated with a gruesome likeness of Paul's severed head. Fad songs with titles such as "St. Paul" by Terry Knight, later producer of Grand Funk Railroad, the ghoulish "Paulbearer," "So Long Paul," recorded by a young Jose Feliciano under the pseudonym Werbley Finster, and "Brother Paul," by Billy Shears and The All-Americans, were released in timely fashion. (Of course the reference to Billy Shears suggested the "imposter" who "stops the show" in the opening strains of the Beatles' "Sgt. Pepper's Lonely Hearts Club Band.") "Brother Paul" was released by WTIX, a New Orleans radio station and had an advance order of 40,000 copies in the New Orleans area alone. (Hockinson, 99). It appeared that a dead Paul McCartney made for very good business!

It was unimaginable that the American public would believe such an unfounded rumor. However, this same generation had been raised on the questionable authority of the infamous Warren Commission report concerning the investigation of John F. Kennedy's assassination. If a conspiracy hiding the facts of an

American president's murder existed, then why would it be out of the realm of possibility for the death of Paul McCartney to be hidden from the public? Just a year before, in 1968, America had lost Bobby Kennedy and Martin Luther King, Jr., two heroic figures, whose deaths many experts believed were the results of conspiracies. So, we questioned everything and we trusted no one—especially those over thirty.

In the meantime, the Beatles had left the safe road of simple love songs and turned to the quest for social awareness. Once clean-cut "good boys," they now strongly opposed the war in Vietnam, and admitted their use of marijuana and LSD. John Lennon had even gone so far as to suggest that the Beatles were more popular than Jesus Christ: "Christianity will go. It will vanish and shrink. I needn't argue about that. I'm right and will be proved right. We're more popular than Jesus Christ now. I don't know which will go first, rock 'n' roll or Christianity. Jesus was all right, but his disciples were thick and ordinary. It's them twisting it that ruins it for me."

The sixties generation desperately needed something to believe in. *Playboy* created a furor when they released statements by the Beatles detailing other questionable beliefs, and made the masses realize for the first time the Beatles weren't the boys next door. At times, the Beatles made what some mothers would consider lewd comments about the *Playboy* playmates appearing in the centerfolds. They claimed that homosexuals could easily be identified in the United States by their crew-cut hair styles. The outrage demonstrated against John's Christianity comments brought forth rumors of Beatles' orgies with underage girls in the Beatles' hotel rooms. Yet again, many of these charges were ridiculous, but it seemed that in some cities, America was in the process of exorcizing its young from the grip of Beatlemania.

Far Eastern influences permeated the Beatles recordings from 1965 to 1967 like the pungent aroma of incense. George Harrison introduced the droning sounds of the sitar into Beatles' compositions. For the first time, the Beatles experimented with backward recordings and introduced metaphysical themes. However, not everyone was happy with this sudden change in the group.

The American public, it seemed, refused to allow change in its heroes. If there really was change in the Beatles, there had to be a reason for it. After the release of the Beatles' albums from 1967 to 1969, those adoring fans of the past became the inquisitors of the present. A scapegoat was demanded, and when the "Paul is dead" rumors surfaced in October 1969, those fans, filled with insecurity, were only too eager to search for the clues that provided the answer for this strange change in the Beatles' behavior.

The answer was obvious: Paul McCartney had indeed died, and an imposter had taken his place.

CHAPTER 2

I
Buried
Paul

THE
SEARCH
FOR
CONSPIRACY

As the public absorbed the many clues to Paul McCartney's supposed death, the first and most obvious task was to examine the possibility of a hidden, mysterious conspiracy. This was not an incredible challenge. Since "the love of money is the root of all evil" (and a man needs roots), the villain had to be either the Beatles themselves or the hated establishment, the people behind the scenes who controlled the bands and profited from their talent.

The Beatles performed their last concert as a group at Candlestick Park in San Francisco on August 19, 1966. After that, the Fab Four became reclusive and seldom appeared in public. They rejected great sums of money to perform live as a pop group once more. The Beatles had become bored with their own notoriety.

According to Ringo, "It was the worst and best time of my life. The best time because we played a lot of good music and had a lot of good times. The worst time . . . where it was like 24 hours a day, without a break: press, people fighting to get into your hotel room, climbing 25 stories up drainpipes. And it never stopped . . . if it had carried on, I personally would have gone insane."

Not every one of the Beatles was convinced about the "good music" to which Ringo referred. In a *Melody Maker* interview, John Lennon exclaimed: "I can't stand listening to most of our early stuff . . . songs like 'Eight Days a Week' and 'She Loves You' sound like big drags to me now. I turn the radio off if they're ever on."

It seemed that the Beatles had given all they possibly could to rock and roll, and now they simply wanted to rest, then change direction. Beatles' albums continued to be released, but with no live tours to support them. The Beatles now started to think of the album as an art form in and of itself, composed of many great songs, not just a showcase of a few hit singles surrounded by album filler. This concept influenced Brian Wilson of the Beach Boys to achieve a similar goal. The result was the release of *Pet Sounds* in 1966, the album that greatly influenced the Beatles' own *Sgt. Pepper's Lonely Hearts Club Band*. McCartney once recalled listening to the lushly produced tracks from *Pet Sounds*, and fearing that the Beatles would never be able to match the creativity of Brian Wilson. In this regard, Wilson's concept album gave the Beatles notice that he, too, could create a *Rubber Soul* or a *Revolver*.

At this time, the making of surrealist and impressionist film fascinated the Beatles. Perhaps to compensate for the lack of live performances, they started releasing film versions of their new hits. These releases included "Hello Goodbye," "Penny Lane," and "Strawberry Fields Forever." The group even financed their own British television film, entitled *Magical Mystery Tour*. This, however, proved to be a monetary disappointment to the band. The Beatles' fans had no idea that the Beatles had given up touring. This was due in great part to the stresses associated with their last American tour, in which John's statements on Christianity caused more than one tense performance. When this was coupled with the disaster in Manila, in which the Beatles unintentionally snubbed the Marcos family and had to leave the country in fear for their lives, it became obvious that they preferred the safety and creative atmosphere of Abbey Road studios.

The public halfheartedly accepted the Beatles' withdrawal from the limelight. If there were to be no more live Beatles' concerts, then at least their fans could still enjoy their music and catch a glimpse of their performances through their avant-garde films. Nonetheless, their withdrawal from the public eye did add fire to the Paul McCartney death rumors.

The public had grown accustomed to the eccentric behavior of popular artists. Fans were only too aware of Elvis' nightmare existence in Memphis, Tennessee. Presley's rental of movie theaters and whole amusement parks after closing time were common knowledge to fans of rock and roll. Fame, it seemed, was not without cost and sacrifice. With this in mind, most of us forgave the Beatles for their reclusiveness.

If the Beatles themselves were off the hook, the next most logical place to look for answers to the McCartney mystery was to the record company executives, the money men who were only concerned with profit, not music. Here were the Andrew Carnegies and J. P. Morgans, men like John D. Rockefeller (whom Andrew Carnegie nicknamed "Wreck a fellow") and Cornelius Vanderbilt (whose family motto became "The public be damned"). Obviously these men, and those like them, were the real ogres behind the conspiracy.

The record industry's equivalent to the "sweat shop" was

the all-night recording session, more frequent due dates for album releases, the soul-tearing grind of endless touring, and a complete disregard for privacy. Had the Beatles been imprisoned behind glittering, golden dollar signs?

Life magazine helped propagate the theory in its November 7, 1969, issue entitled "The Magical McCartney Mystery," written by John Neary. If the rumors were true that Paul McCartney had died in a mysterious automobile accident then, perhaps, Neary wrote, the Beatles' management, record companies, and publishing companies conspired to cover up his untimely death. After all, Paul McCartney, dubbed "the cute Beatle," was extremely popular. If Paul was really gone, how were the businessmen going to keep the records selling? Would the public accept a secret replacement for one of the English messiahs? It was farfetched, but not inconceivable.

The Beach Boys had tried to replace Brian Wilson with Glenn Campbell during one of their tours, before settling on Bruce Johnson as a permanent replacement. Wilson had undergone a nervous breakdown and a drug dependency that necessitated such a change. Strangely, some Beach Boys' insiders say it was the Beatles' release of *Sgt. Pepper's Lonely Hearts Club Band* that brought about Wilson's breakdown. His depression grew as, for days, he listened constantly to the Beatles' masterpiece through his stereo headphones. Perhaps he also wondered how he could ever top *Pet Sounds* and meet the Beatles' new musical challenge. But, without Wilson, the Beach Boys seemed to lose the old magic of "I Get Around" and "Surfer Girl." The Rolling Stones had replaced Brian Jones with Mick Taylor. Taylor was an incredible talent, but the music was just not the same. Though the Stones produced, and continue to produce, great music, the fire of "Jumpin' Jack Flash" and "Satisfaction" was not rekindled.

Given these examples, the risk of publicly replacing a dead McCartney may have been considered too great. Surely, the remaining Beatles could continue their music behind locked studio doors and keep quiet about the conspiracy that now hid the death of McCartney. After all, the Beatles stood to gain tremendous sums of money from the royalties of future albums. But, what if the Beatles were not profiteers? What if the Beatles wanted to be true to their fans?

The group had unquestionably undergone a metamorphosis; was it because they were trying to spread the truth to the fans and let them in on the grisly facts? If so, these revelations manifested themselves in a series of cryptic clues. Some clues were shrouded in the lyrics of Beatles' songs, other clues were hidden on Beatles' album covers. All fans had to do was look carefully, have a good imagination, a fair knowledge of Far Eastern and mythological symbolism, and, most important, have the money to purchase the albums in question. The search was on and the answers were forthcoming.

CHAPTER 3

I
Buried
Paul

THE
FATAL
ACCIDENT

*"Wednesday morning
At five o'clock as
The day begins"*
—*"She's Leaving Home"*

On June 1, 1967, the Beatles released *Sgt. Pepper's Lonely Hearts Club Band*. Possibly no other album in history brought about as much change in musical direction as this work. It ushered in a new era, filled with psychedelic sounds that drenched our imaginations in shades of fluorescent colors and pulsating rhythms. After the first week, the album had sold over two hundred fifty thousand units. In the United States, advance sales numbered one million units and, after three months, American sales reached an amazing 2.5 million. By mid-1987, the album's twentieth anniversary, *Sgt. Pepper's Lonely Hearts Club Band* had sold 15 million copies (Dowlding, 153).

Paul McCartney was convinced that *Sgt. Pepper's* was a great artistic album, and insisted that the album's cover should match that greatness. After all, the album took more than seven hundred hours to record and cost about seventy-five thousand dollars (Dowlding, 154). Peter Blake, who created the artwork for the album, stated: "Paul explained [that the concept] was like a band you might see in a park." The cover shot would be a photograph of them as though they were a town band finishing a concert in a park, playing on a bandstand with a municipal flower bed next to it, with a crowd of people gathered around them. "I think my main contribution was to decide that if we made the crowd a certain way, the people in it could be anybody."

The Beatles did not want just anyone to be among the crowd. The cast included such famous and infamous characters as Marilyn Monroe, Aleister Crowley (The Beast 666), Mae West, Edgar Allen Poe, Oliver Hardy, Karl Marx, Lewis Carroll, Johnny Weissmuller, and Shirley Temple. When the Beatles' management sought releases from the individuals pictured on the album cover, Mae West responded, "What would I be doing in a lonely heart's club band?" All four Beatles wrote West personal letters detailing how much they wanted her to appear on the album. Mae West then agreed and took her place on the cover with the other notables (Dowlding, 157).

Not all the Beatles' choices made it to the cover, however. John Lennon had suggested that Ghandi, Jesus Christ, and Hitler be included. Through the intervention of Brian Epstein and EMI records, those suggestions were denied. Possibly the Beatles' management remembered the public's reaction to Lennon's remarks that the Beatles were more popular than Christ. Therefore, it was important not to risk offending the Christians, Hindus, and Jews, so those figures were removed from the set. Actor Leo Gorcey, one of the Bowery Boys, was taken out of the scene when he demanded a fee. Originally, Gorcey was positioned between the Vargas girl and fellow Bowery Boy Huntz Hall.

On the cover, the Beatles dressed in band uniforms, all distinctly different colors, and gathered around a bass drum bearing the album title. Each band member held a different instrument. These instruments required a total of four hours of careful polishing (Dowlding, 157). It seemed that such a visual masterpiece required strict detail to even the smallest items.

As death clue investigators pored ever-so-cautiously over each minuscule detail of *Sgt. Pepper's* album cover, a number of surprising and bizarre images stood out. The group stood in the center of the montage. Immediately to the right of the performers stood their wax figures, the same effigies that resided in Madame Tussaud's wax museum in London. The Beatle likenesses were dressed in the fab style of the sixties—ties, collarless jackets, the famous moptop hairstyle—but for some reason the once-infamous haircut now appeared too conservative. American culture had changed so dramatically that even those individuals over thirty now wore longer hairstyles that made even the Beatles' look of 1964 seem square.

The wax figures stood together next to the likeness of Sonny Liston, and gazed downward toward the freshly dug grave covered in red hyacinths that spelled out *Beatles*. Peter Blake offered this description from the liner notes of *Sgt. Pepper's* CD edition. Blake had the idea of including the wax images of the early Beatles so as to make them a part of the crowd gathered together to witness the birth and new direction of *Sgt. Pepper's*. Blake explained how the "Welcome the Rolling Stones" sweatshirt came from Michael Cooper's young son, Adam. The interesting origin of the yellow-hyacinth-flowered guitar is described simply as a gift from a young Beatles' fan who wished to contribute to the album artwork. The Beatles arrived for the photo shoot on the evening of March 30 and, in three hours, all the shots were finished. This included the cover, the centerfold, and the back cover. When questioned about the cost of the project, Blake commented that he received two hundred pounds for the set design, and that photographer Robert Fraser was paid fifteen hundred pounds by EMI. Even though this does not sound like a great deal of money for such a historic project, Blake was only too happy to contribute his creation to rock history.

The cover photograph offered a number of sinister clues. The spectators, perhaps, represented the mourners at a funeral. It did not take long to ascertain that the beautiful yellow hyacinths were in the shape of a left-handed bass guitar, McCartney's instrument. The presence of Stu Sutcliffe in the crowd may suggest that the instrument placed on the grave actually belonged to him. Sutcliffe, the first Beatles' bassist and Lennon's best friend, died of a brain hemorrhage in Germany shortly before the Beatles' rise to rock stardom. If the viewer looked carefully, and used a little imagination, he could make out the macabre message "Paul?" from the hyacinths. Onlookers also noticed that there were only three black strings on the instrument. Was this a reference to the three mourning Beatles?

The flower Beatles arrangement also represented a clue to many fans—some of whom believed they could make out the numeral three before Beatles. Could this yet again suggest the three surviving members?

Many fans suggested that the lone word *Beatles* spelled out in red hyacinths may have suggested that those figures present were only some of the band members (perhaps along with a very lucky imposter). Also interesting is that on a number of later Beatles' albums (*Magical Mystery Tour, Abbey Road,* and *Let It Be*) the band refers to itself as "Beatles," as opposed to "the Beatles." To many investigators, it appeared that by not labeling themselves *the* Beatles, the group gave one more clue that the band was not in its original formation.

To those onlookers with a more active imagination, the blood-red hyacinth message read "Be at Leso." The obscure *o* helped form the enigmatic name of a certain Greek Island, rumored to have been purchased by the Beatles themselves for the final resting place of Paul McCartney. To make matters even more complicated, this incredible island was said to have been underwater. Perhaps overzealous fans combined the myth of McCartney's death with the ancient wonder of another sunken island—Atlantis. As mentioned earlier, some clues bordered on the ridiculous and could not possibly hold water. But, then again, maybe the island was converted into a home for legendary performers who many believed faked their own deaths. The inhabitants could have included James Dean, Jim Morrison, and a now-tan Elvis waiting for his comeback tour in 2001!

Strangely, at the 1995 Chicago *Beatlefest*, Alistair Taylor mentioned a bizarre story in which John Lennon had asked him to purchase an island. The next day, he saw an advertisement offering an island for sale. One wonders if Lennon perhaps named this island "Leso," or if this was merely another one of his gags.

Issy Bonn, a British comedian, and a member of the crowd who adorned the album jacket, had his right hand raised above Paul McCartney's head. Supposedly, in certain Far Eastern societies, an upraised hand held over the head of a subject was a symbol of death, or a symbol of religious benediction associated with funerals. At the very least, McCartney was singled out from the others in this strange manner.

While McCartney stood under the open hand, three of the performers (John, Ringo, and George) held bright, golden, band instruments. McCartney, on the other hand, held a black clarinet. Symbolically, black has always represented mourning or death. Another clue presented on the album cover concerned the curly-haired Shirley Temple doll placed at George Harrison's left, looking down upon the grave. The doll wore a striped "Welcome the Rolling Stones" sweatshirt. This intent to plug the Rolling Stones was rather obvious, and the Stones later returned the favor by placing the Beatles' likenesses among the shrubs on *Their Satanic Majesties Request*. But, under closer examination, investigators noticed a small model car resting on the doll's right leg. This model car strongly resembled an Aston Martin, the mysterious car McCartney supposedly drove on the ill-fated night of November 9, 1966, the date of his purported accident. The doll sat in the lap of a macabre grandmother figure, wearing what appeared to be a blood-stained driving glove on her left hand. Strangely, since McCartney was left-handed, this was interpreted as yet another reference that Paul had been involved in a tragic accident.

Investigators also took delight in noticing a flowerlike arrangement, peculiarly resembling a flaming car pushed head-first into the grave. The Indian goddess Kali was placed directly front and center of the album jacket. Kali, an Eastern religious symbol of rebirth and regeneration, was described in G. A. Gaskell's *Dictionary of All Scriptures and Myths* as "a symbol of the present period and process of evolution in which wisdom and love are gradually developed from ignorance and desire. This period of evolution of spirit from matter commences from the death of the Archetypal man (Krishna)."

The Beatles' McCartney could have been that archetypal man, joining the ranks of literary heroes who died young and were later reborn as gods, like Achilles or Alexander. This may have paralleled Lennon's statement that the Beatles were more popular than Christ. Only, this time, Lennon could have been answering his fundamentalist detractors through symbolic images. In this symbolic state McCartney may have represented a Christ figure born again not for the spiritual redemption of mankind, but raised like the Phoenix from the ashes of ignorance and intolerance to lead the way to wisdom and love. Remember this was 1967, San Francisco was in the midst of the Summer of Love celebration, and all things were possible.

John Lennon was strongly influenced by Lewis Carroll: "My influences are tremendous, from Lewis Carroll to Oscar Wilde to tough little kids that use to live next to me who ended up in prison and things like that" (Scheff, 140). It seemed that the Beatles shared the same passion for word play that Carroll used as a staple in his works.

With Carroll's *Through the Looking Glass* in mind, I experimented with a small, flat mirror held at an angle to certain spots on *Sgt. Pepper's* cover. I became particularly interested in the bass drum, when I read that the designer was a mysterious Joe Ephgrave. The last name surely was a combination of *epitaph* and *grave*.

The bass drum skin looked, at first, innocent enough, with the album title psychedelically etched across its surface. The two phrases *Sgt. Pepper's* and *Club Band* were angled to the top and bottom of the drumhead and in similar design. The phrase *Lonely Hearts* was of a different lettering, and placed in the center. The different pattern appeared awkward. Why wasn't the same lettering used for the complete album title? In researching the making of *Sgt. Pepper's*, it was determined that there were two bass drum skins designed for the cover. The second drum skin contains a different motif, except for the exact placement of the phrase *Lonely Hearts*. The mysterious lettering had to present some hidden clue. If there is a smoking gun to suggest the Beatles' involvement of placing concealed clues to Paul's supposed death it was here.

By holding the mirror perpendicular to the cover and in the dead center of "Lonely Hearts," a hidden message appeared between the glass and cover. The message read: "I One IX He ◊ Die." Between the words "he" and "die" was a diamond-shaped arrow pointing upward to McCartney!

At first the nine (IX) was obscure. Initially, I assumed it meant that the Beatle with nine letters in his name had died, which fit nicely, since only McCartney's name contained the needed nine letters.

Dissatisfied with this explanation, I sought an answer to the first mark, the "I One." I read the phrase over and over as "one one nine he die," which was extremely frustrating, until I realized that, unlike in mathematics, one and one must not always equal two. In this case, one and one was eleven!

Now the phrase was "Eleven Nine He ◊ Die" and the answer was obvious. The bass drum became the true tombstone and revealed the exact date of death: November ninth—the eleventh month and ninth day.

As mentioned earlier, there is evidence to support the theory that Paul McCartney had been involved in an accident on November 9, 1966. The incredible revelation, however, was that some wanted us to believe that McCartney had died and the album jacket simply served as an obituary to the unsuspecting world.

But the mystery did not end there! The hidden message in the bass drum may have been designed only for American audiences. The European method for dates places the day followed by the month, then the year. In this case, the message would appear to an English audience as "nine one one" or September eleventh.

In the open album jacket, the Beatles appeared in a closeup shot still dressed in their *Sgt. Pepper's* uniforms. On his left arm, McCartney wore an arm patch that read "OPD." While in the United States an individual who has died in an accident and been rushed to the nearest hospital is pronounced dead on arrival or DOA, in England, the corresponding term is OPD or officially pronounced dead—the exact acronym that adorned McCartney's left arm. Paul McCartney later answered the critics' interpretation of the arm patch with a statement suggesting that the Beatles obtained the insignia in Canada and that it "possibly" could have stood for Ontario Police Department.

Actually, the patch represented Ontario Provincial Police (OPP), yet it seems odd that McCartney would forget the exact lettering of the infamous badge, especially in trying to discredit any sinister connotation. Also in the center section of the album jacket, McCartney is the only Beatle sitting in what many fans quickly interpreted as the fetal position—the same manner in which the ancient Celts buried their dead.

The pulses of sleuths must have raced feverishly upon looking at the back of the *Sgt. Pepper's Lonely Hearts Club Band* album cover. The most noticeable clue was McCartney posed with his back to the camera, while the other Beatles faced the lens with stern expressions. Again, McCartney was singled out and portrayed differently from the others. Some of the more overzealous fans believed that the imposter had to turn his back to the camera simply to avoid being recognized as a fake. Those same fans noticed that the McCartney likeness appeared unnaturally stiff. Was this but a three dimensional cutout? Upon closer inspection, wasn't McCartney holding a black wooden instrument? (If you look carefully, he places three fingers of his left hand at the base of the instrument. Was this another attempt to hint at three Beatles?) In this photograph, Paul didn't quite fit in as a member of a brass marching band.

The album jacket's back side was bright red, which led many to think that this represented the accidental spilling of McCartney's blood. (Some of the more ghoulish investigators noticed that the original album sleeves appeared to be blood-stained, as though the sleeves had been used to absorb a pool of blood.)

This was also the first time in history that an album's lyrics were included with the recording. The title that appeared across Paul's back was the song "Within You Without You," a song penned by George Harrison, containing the lyrics: "We were talking—about the space between us all / And the people—who hide themselves behind a wall of illusion / Never glimpse the truth—then it's far too late—when they pass away." This lyric appeared to be prophetic. Who were these "people who hide themselves behind a wall of illusion"? What was the mysterious "truth"? Yet again, who had "passed away"? Did this mean that the Beatles would go on with Paul or without him?

Since it was George's song, it was appropriate that he should reveal the next hidden meaning. Harrison stood to McCartney's right. As he faced the photographer, George pointed somberly to a superimposed line from "She's Leaving Home." The lyric read: "Wednesday morning at five o'clock as the day begins." To ensure the validity of the accident theory, researchers consulted a calender from 1966 and found that November 9, 1966, was indeed a Wednesday and that McCartney's accident had occurred at 5:00 A.M. (Dowlding, 158).

One surprising bit of information concerning Paul's alleged involvement in a tragic automobile accident is reportedly found in the *Beatles Book Monthly*, February 1967. The article mentions a rumor circulating through London stating that on January 7, 1967, the roads around London became icy and very dangerous. Late that afternoon, it was reported that Paul McCartney had been killed in a car crash on the M1 Motorway. As this supposition fueled an hysterical outpouring from Beatles' fans, one of the Beatles' press agents placed a call to Paul at his

St. John's Wood home. The Beatle confirmed that he had been home all day and had not left the house. Since there was no truth to the report, the story died there. What is peculiar to the story, however, is the time frame. Since *Sgt. Pepper's* was in the early stages of production at this time, could this hysteria have been the catalyst for Paul and the other Beatles to plant the "Paul is dead" rumors? Obviously, after the many frantic calls seeking the truth about Paul's accident, the Beatles would have been aware of such an incredible marketing strategy. All they had to do was present the story in detailed yet cryptic clues, to the unsuspecting world! Remember, *Sgt. Pepper's* was released in Great Britain and the United States in June 1967, thus leaving plenty of time to create the world's greatest hoax.

Upon closer examination, onlookers noticed that the Beatles had placed their epaulets upon their left shoulders, said to be the proper attire for military honor guards at state funerals. Interestingly, the Beatles had consciously changed the epaulets from their right to left shoulders, which is evident by comparing the front and back LP covers. It is also interesting to note that the term *epaulet* contains Paul's name (ePAULet). Also, Paul wears three black buttons on his jacket. Possibly symbols of the three surviving Beatles who mourned their partner's tragic end.

Other clues hinting tragic deaths through automobile accidents were hidden within Beatles' song lyrics, the most prevalent of which was found in *Sgt. Pepper's* haunting "A Day in the Life." According to John Lennon: "I was reading the paper one day and noticed two stories. One was about the Guinness heir who killed himself in a car. That was the main headline story. He died in London in a car crash. On the next page was a story about four thousand potholes in the streets of Blackburn, Lancashire, that needed to be filled. Paul's contribution was the beautiful little lick, 'I'd love to turn you on,' that he'd had float-ing around in his head and couldn't use. I thought it was a damn good piece of work" (Sheff, 163).

The Guinness heir that Lennon referred to was Tara Browne, the same figure who was with Paul at the time of his moped accident, and was a friend of the Beatles and other Eng-lish groups. On December 18, 1966, Browne sped through red traffic lights at 110 miles per hour in his Lotus Elan, and smashed into the back of a van parked in South Kensington. He was dead at the age of twenty-one (Dowlding, 179-80).

As to the line "I'd love to turn you on," McCartney stated, "I remember being very conscious of the words 'I'd love to turn you on' and thinking, 'Well, that's about as risque as we dare get at this point.' Well, the BBC banned it" (*Playboy*, December 1984).

In the lyrics to "A Day in the Life," Lennon mentions read-ing a newspaper account of a terrible accident where someone "blows his mind out in a car" as he enters an intersection against the light. A crowd of onlookers soon appears that have seen the victim's face before.

Obviously, the death in question had to concern that of an individual who was extremely well-known. In Peter Brown and Stephen Gaines' *The Love You Make: An Insider's Story of the Beatles*, the authors referred to this scene: "It was actually John Lennon who 'blew his mind out in a car.' John and Terry Doran were driving into London from Weybridge one night with John at the wheel, so stoned on acid he couldn't figure out if the traf-fic light had changed" (Brown and Gaines, 373).

The "crowd of people" who "stood and stared" may have represented an older generation who had seen the face of the dead man somewhere—probably in the newspapers or on tele-vision—but couldn't readily identify the corpse. The word "nobody" may have been used to describe the body as a victim of decapitation ("blew his mind out") and, with grim humor, allude to the fact that the head had "no body."

In prehistoric times and in many tribal societies, the head was considered to be the receptacle of the spirit (Cirlot, 78). If the head were removed, the spirit could then be freed and, in this case, perhaps bring about a transition to the idealistic concepts of wisdom and love contained in a higher plane of existence. This grim irony would fit Lennon's statement that he "just had to laugh" at the rather sad news in the newspaper. The meaning behind this phrase suggested Lennon's awareness of the humor hidden behind his carefully chosen words. If "a crowd of people stood and stared" at the body, this line could refer to *Sgt. Pepper's* artwork, containing the crowd of people, and fellow celebrities, who now served as members of a wake.

The crowd gathered around a grave has ghoulishly identified the victim for the viewer. However, the record-buying public knew that being a Beatle was much more prestigious than being a simple member of the House of Lords. Many clue seekers were convinced that Lennon actually sang "nobody was really sure if he was from the House of Paul." Again, this could be another episode of simple coincidence, but this lyric seemed to fit the phrase more closely than the cover lyric sheet which stated "Nobody was really sure / If he was from the House of Lords."

After the public was made aware of the car-crash clue from "A Day in the Life," fans were prompted to ponder lyrics from past Beatle recordings. The Beatles' album *Help!* showed McCartney as the only Beatle without a hat—yet again being portrayed differently from his fellow bandmates.

The album *Rubber Soul* now induced images of screaming tires (rubber) and death (soul), leading many sleuths to think that McCartney had died during the making of this album. It seemed irrelevant that the album was released in the United Kingdom on December 3, 1965, and in the United States on December 6, 1965, almost a year before the tragic accident was said to have occurred. These newfound mourners searched for any and all clues that would help shed light upon the McCartney mystery. By this point, some of us saw only what we wanted to see, and heard only what we wanted to hear. Most people completely ignored Lennon's comment that the album title came from a pun on "English soul" (Dowlding, 113). The death-clue answer made much more sense.

There could well be another pun interpreted as yet another clue to McCartney's death. *Sgt. Pepper's* contains the first mention of Apple. The Beatles note that this side of the album cover was designed by "M.C. Productions and the Apple." The M.C. productions could well refer to McCartney, while "apple," when divided into two syllables, forms another cryptic clue. The first syllable, the prefix *a*, could mean "without" (as in areligious, apolitical, etc.). When the prefix *a* is used in front of the second syllable *pple*, the phrase could be translated as *a-pple*, or without Paul.

The American release of *The Beatles Yesterday . . . and Today* in June, 1966, supposedly contained other clues to McCartney's tragic death. John Lennon described the controversy behind the jacket: "The original cover was the Beatles in white coats with figs 'n' dead bits of meat and dolls cut up. It was inspired by our boredom and resentment at having to do another photo session and another Beatle thing. We were sick to death of it. Also, the photographer was into Dali and making surreal pictures. That combination produced that cover" (Sheff, 194).

The cover was deemed in poor taste by the Beatles' management and a substitute photograph was pasted directly over the offending picture. The new album jacket displayed the group posed by an open trunk. Paul McCartney sat inside the trunk, interpreted by many fans as an open coffin—especially when the album was turned on its side.

To the most ardent believers of Beatles' conspiracy, the album photo represented the ultimate theory of a coverup, since the original art was recalled and a new photo pasted hastily in its place. What was the true purpose of such an act? Did the Butcher Cover suggest other clues to Paul's desmise?

On the original cover photograph, Paul is sitting in the middle of the first row between John and Ringo, and is surrounded on either side by headless dolls. Paul laughingly grips one of the dolls' heads in his lap while George tries to place another doll's head upon a headless body. To some onlookers, this was yet another clue to Paul's accident. Also, it is interesting to note a pair of false teeth upon Paul's right forearm. To the more persistent seekers of the truth, this clue reinforced a cryptic passage in "Revolution 9": "So any and all, he went to see the dentist instead, who gave him a pair of teeth, which wasn't any good at all." My friend Jay Fox from the ABC Radio Network mentioned to me that it is possible to make out the actual time displayed on Paul's wristwatch. According to Jay, the time can be read as 5:05, possibly a reference to the line "Wednesday morning at five o'clock" from "She's Leaving Home" included on *Sgt. Pepper's*. (It is also interesting to note that on *Sgt. Pepper's* there is yet another reference to five o'clock. In the song "Good Morning, Good Morning, Lennon sings, "People running round it's five o'clock. / Everywhere in town is getting dark / Everyone you see is full of life." Ironically, the first line of "Good Morning, Good Morning" states "Nothing to do to save his life." In this case the phrase "Good Morning" may suggest a play on the words *morning* and *mourning*.

The very title *Yesterday . . . and Today* may have suggested that the photo represented the Beatles as we remembered them in the past (yesterday), whereas this photograph portrayed the group as they are today, with an imposter taking the place of Paul. A number of song titles on the album could also be interpreted as references to the supposed rumor. The album opened with "Drive My Car" (was this a reference to McCartney's accident?); "I'm Only Sleeping" (a reference to Paul in an unmarked grave?); "Dr. Robert" (though this song was written about a drug supplier, it could have suggested the mysterious doctor who signed Paul's death certificate and went along with the conspiracy); "Yesterday" (the way the Beatles were before McCartney's tragic end); "Act Naturally" (the way the Beatles have gone on, pretending that Paul was still alive); "If I Needed Someone" (did the Beatles need a replacement for Paul to complete the band?); and "We Can Work It Out" (a reference to the Beatles and their management promoting the coverup of Paul's death).

Today, the original *Yesterday . . . and Today* with the Butcher Cover is a collector's item, valued in the thousands. Of course, for many collectors, the cover must be carefully steamed away to reveal this hidden prize, perhaps suggesting another clue to encourage the public to examine each Beatles' product carefully to find the truth. Besides, Lennon mentioned that the Beatles were bored. This ruse could have given them an outlet to provide further clues to a tragic death, and didn't John once state that Americans would buy anything?

Parlophone re-released a collection of Beatle hits for the British market in December 1966. This import is called *A Collection of Beatle Oldies.* This album was released in Great Britain on December 10, 1966, immediately preceding *Sgt. Pepper's,* and may have included the first clues to the "Paul is dead" rumors.

The cover shows the Beatles in the upper left-hand corner, posed by a convertible. One of the figures, who resembles Paul to some degree, is holding a cigarette in his right hand (McCartney was a natural lefty; this clue is later repeated on the *Abbey Road* cover). There is a large blowup of a Beatle figure sitting on a bass drum that proclaims OLDIES in large capital letters. The drawing also shows a car with its headlights on (representing a late-night drive, or a drive, perhaps, on a Wednesday morning at 5 o'clock) heading off the road in what appears to be a collision course with the large Beatle figure's head. Remember, the rumor suggested that Paul had died from decapitation or from a serious head injury. The larger-than-life figure is dressed in mod clothing and the face is shadowed. It is odd that this is the only area that is shadowed on the entire body.

This could well suggest Robert Freeman's cover photo for the album *With the Beatles* in which shadows play a dominant role in each Beatle's facial photograph. There is a strange coincidence between the two covers concerning the placement of the shadowed face. On the *Oldies* cover the Beatle figure's head is in the upper-right corner of the album jacket, the exact location of Paul McCartney's photograph on the *With the Beatles* cover.

Since a bass drum provided such an incredible clue on *Sgt. Pepper's* cover, perhaps there would be another hidden message on the *Oldies* drum skin. Notice that the last four letters in *Oldies* are *dies*. Then, if the letters O and L are advanced one letter each, we get the letters P and M. When the phrase is read together it appears to suggest P (Paul) M (McCartney) Dies. (Many of Arthur C. Clarke's fans noted that Clarke may have provided the same cryptic puzzle in the naming of his killer computer system in *2001: A Space Odyssey*. The system's name was HAL.

If each letter is raised one letter in sequence the reader will become aware of a rather famous maker of computers. Of course, this may be just another strange coincidence.)

In the back-cover photograph, Paul is the only Beatle dressed in black. To some, the large figure resting upon the bass drum may suggest McCartney's replacement, a replacement whose facial features resemble none of the actual members of the Beatles, but instead bear the features of a complete stranger. This may be a stretch, but it is a work of great imagination, something the Beatles certainly didn't lack.

CHAPTER 4

The
Imposter
Theory

SGT. PEPPER'S
LONELY HEARTS
CLUB BAND

"Let me introduce to you
The one and only
Billy Shears"
—"Sgt. Pepper's Lonely Hearts
Club Band"

As Beatles' fans searched diligently for more clues to the great "Paul is dead" mystery, it became popular to re-examine the Beatles' album that laid the psychedelic foundation for *Sgt. Pepper's*. That album, of course, was *Revolver*. *Revolver* was released in England on August 5, 1966, and in the United States on August 8, 1966. *Revolver* included "Got to Get You into My Life" which featured the opening lyric: "I was alone. / I took a ride. / I didn't know what I would find there." Could this line have also referred to Paul's mysterious death? Surely not, since the Beatles were preparing to leave on the tour that later proved to be their last. To be significant to the car crash, all clues must come after the Candlestick Park concert. Obviously, some fans jumped at any clue that may have suggested the fatal crash, or Paul's being alone and not knowing that he was very close to the hereafter.

The song "She Said She Said" contained a line: "I know what it's like to be dead." In the *Playboy Interviews*, Lennon recalled that "She Said She Said" was "written after an acid trip in L.A. during a break in the Beatles' tour [August 1965] where we were having fun with the Byrds and lots of girls . . . Peter Fonda came in when we were on acid and he kept coming up to me and sitting next to me and whispering 'I know what it's like to be dead.' He was describing an acid trip he had been on. We didn't want to hear about that! We were on an acid trip and the sun was shining and the girls were dancing and the whole thing was beautiful and sixties, and this guy—who I really didn't know; he hadn't made *Easy Rider* or anything—kept coming over, wearing shades, saying, 'I know what it's like to be dead,' and we kept leaving him because he was so boring! And I used it for the song, but I changed it to 'she' not 'he.' It was scary. You know, a guy . . . when you're flying high and [whispers] 'I know what it's like to be dead, man.' I remembered the incident. Don't tell me about it! I don't want to know what it's like to be dead" (Sheff, 160).

Devoted followers of the macabre decided that the gender change was only another attempt at keeping the tragedy from the public. The word *revolver* evoked images of change. Just as the cylinder turns in a handgun, or revolver, for the purpose of loading a new cartridge, so might the Beatles have moved to replace a fallen member with a substitute. The album cover displayed McCartney's likeness in profile, suggesting that his picture was pieced into the drawing with the other members. No matter how absurd these clues sounded, the public had a field day as they searched through their old Beatles' albums and read double meanings into every line of every lyric. No one will ever know for sure just how many turntables were ruined by overzealous fans who turned the platters backward and destroyed the delicate mechanisms inside the players.

If the visual clues could be taken literally, and Paul McCartney actually died in an automobile accident on November 9, 1966, then who was the mysterious Paul on *Sgt. Pepper's* cover? When the death rumors circulated throughout the press, fans and other sleuths formulated somewhat incredible theories about the identity of the imposter Beatle. Some sources claimed that Paul was an actor named William Campbell. Campbell was supposedly the winner of a Paul McCartney lookalike contest and, conveniently, an orphan from Edinburgh. Campbell allegedly went so far as to have plastic surgery to make himself resemble McCartney even more closely (Dowlding, 158). Of course, it didn't hurt to assume that Campbell could write the same types of songs as the real McCartney, and just happened to have a voice that was also identical.

Under closer investigation, researchers found a Campbelltown a few miles from Paul's home at Highgate. Perhaps this suggested another clue to the imposter's identity. However, a number of sleuths reasoned that if an impostor had taken McCartney's place, then that must been the reason for the Beatles' ending their live performances. After all, it would have taken a great deal of time for a stand-in to have counterfeited the true Paul's performance. No one in the Beatles' camp would have wanted to risk becoming aware of the coverup when they attended Beatles' concerts. Some overzealous fans noticed a strange picture of McCartney in disguise pasted on the liner sheet from the White Album. These fans were convinced that the Beatles were brazen enough to have actually printed a photograph of the look-alike in his natural appearance.

Another interesting controversy surrounded the true identity of the man in the blue band uniform on the back of *Sgt. Pepper's*. Though some Beatle insiders claimed that it was actually McCartney in the poses, Neville Stannard's *The Long and Winding Road: A History of the Beatles on Record* suggested that the mysterious Paul was Mal Evans, a Beatles' road manager. Stannard suggested that McCartney had made plans to be with his girlfriend, Jane Asher, in the United States to help celebrate her twenty-first birthday, making him unavailable for the photo sessions. So, Evans took his place, but with his back facing the camera. In this case, there was enough evidence to support the supposition of a Beatle imposter. Of course, many observers noticed that there were photos of McCartney included in the 1987 twentieth-anniversary release of the *Sgt. Pepper's* CD, striking a similar pose with his back to the camera. Believers in the conspiracy theory were convinced that the double was forced to turn his back to the camera to hide the scars from recent plastic surgery. Imagine their excitement when they noticed the scar above Paul's lip in the "Paperback Writer" video (complete with missing tooth), and also on his individual photo from the White Album.

As the lines of *Sgt. Pepper's* title song rang out through our stereo speakers, we heard the singer (Paul McCartney) declare, "I don't really want to stop the show," and then "So let me introduce to you / The one and only Billy Shears / And Sgt. Pepper's Lonely Hearts Club Band." Why did Paul McCartney not want to stop the show? Did this mean that with the death of the popular Beatle, the road to riches and further glory would then be over for the three remaining group members, as well as for their record companies, publishing companies, and management? Does McCartney actually go as far as to introduce his double? Who was this mysterious Billy Shears?

One of the most fascinating rumors of this period dealt with a mysterious Beatle look-alike contest in the early sixties. The Paul McCartney look-alike winner's photograph was never published, but the rumor spread that his name was released as

Billy Shears. Billy Shears could well have been a pseudonym for William Campbell. McCartney mentioned that the Beatles used the name Billy Shears only for its "poetic ring." Death-clue advocates then proposed that this was the Beatles' first introduction of the substitute. Lee Merrick wrote an article for *The Rat Subterranean News* that suggested the Billy Shears imposter theory on October 29, 1969. Merrick also stated that the imposter's father was Philip Shears, who lived in Chelsea. It seems that Fred LaBour was the first to credit William Campbell as the winner of the mysterious look-alike contest. Though it was not unusual to have Beatle look-alike contests in every country around the world, the name William Campbell seems to only have served as an attempt for enthusiasts to help spread the McCartney mystery.

When the first song, "Sgt. Pepper's," faded into the next composition, "A Little Help from My Friends," the listener heard the band sing "Billeee Shears!"(Of course, some of the overzealous claimed to hear the phrase, "Billy's here," suggesting the arrival of the Beatle imposter.) One of Ringo's first lines in this number was "Lend me your ears and I'll sing you a song / And I'll try not to sing out of key." Why would one of the Beatles have to worry about singing out of key? Was this a reference to a hidden insecurity that the public would not accept a replacement in the popular group?

Upon closer listening, it sounded almost like an apology to the audience. The chorus stated that the singer would get by with a little help from his friends, and was going to try with a little help from his friends. Perhaps these lines referred to the coverup in which the imposter maintained his hidden existence only through the help of his friends—in this case, the Beatles and their management. This seemed a distinct possibility, or at least sounded plausible. Perhaps this was only another piece of the puzzle that had become one of the greatest mysteries in music history.

Sgt. Pepper's was recognized as "a new and golden renaissance of song" by *The New York Review of Books.* Timothy Leary, LSD apostle, described the album: "The *Sgt. Pepper's* album . . . compresses the evolutionary development of musicology and much of the history of Eastern and Western sound in a new tympanic complexity. The Beatles are Divine Messiahs. Prototypes of a new young race of laughing free men" (Dowlding, 162).

It seemed that the world had ironically taken Dr. Leary's famous suggestion to "Turn on, tune in, and drop out." David Crosby of the Byrds and later of Crosby, Stills, Nash and Young fame stated: "Somehow *Sgt. Pepper's* did not stop the Vietnam War. Somehow it didn't work. Somebody isn't listening . . . I would've thought *Sgt. Pepper's* could've stopped the war just by putting too many good vibes in the air for anybody to have a war around" (Dowlding, 163).

But all was not lost. While it was true that mankind was still not ready for the message of peace and harmony that the album extolled, *Sgt. Pepper's* did manage to stand as the greatest rock album of all time as voted by critics and broadcasters in Paul Gambaccini's *The Top 100 Rock and Roll Albums of All Time.* It won in both the 1977 and 1987 editions.

Sgt. Pepper's Lonely Hearts Club Band also illustrated that the Beatles maintained a sense of humor. At the conclusion of the recording, a high-frequency note at about 18 kilocycles per second was originally added to the second side of the album. It is inaudible to humans, but dogs can hear it. A few seconds of gibberish were included on the run-out groove. McCartney suggested it for the benefit of people who had a turntable that didn't shut off. The needle would go around and around in the groove without shutting off, and some gibberish in that groove was deemed better than hiss. Some listeners thought that the gibberish said, "Lucy Abbey all the way," or "He's found heaven." When the tape is reversed, a voice is said to say, "We'll all be back here soon." This could well be a Freudian nightmare!

When Paul McCartney talked to journalist Paul Gambaccini in December, 1973, he told this story about the hidden meaning: "I went inside . . . and played it studiously, turned it backwards with my thumb against the motor, turned the motor off and did it backwards. And there it was, plain as anything, 'We'll fuck you like Supermen.' I thought, Jesus, what can you do?" (*Rolling Stone* January 31, 1974; Hockinson, 99).

Recording the two seconds of gibberish took a full night, from seven at night to three in the morning, more than half the time it took to record the Beatles' entire first album *Please Please Me* (Dowlding, 160). Recording engineer Geoff Emerick and producer George Martin calculated that the *Sgt. Pepper's* album took a total of seven hundred hours to complete, whereas *Please Please Me* took a grand total of 585 minutes.

CHAPTER 5

The Mystery of the *Magical Mystery Tour*

"What? is he dead?
Goo goo g'joob."
—*"I Am the Walrus"*

 The search for more clues to the untimely demise of Paul McCartney continued with the release of *Magical Mystery Tour* on December 8, 1967, in Great Britain, as a soundtrack to the Beatles' film of the same name. *Magical Mystery Tour* included a twenty-four-page booklet of stills from the film. The United States release was on November 27, 1967, and included Beatles singles from 1967 like "Hello Goodbye." Some of the new songs were actually written for *Sgt. Pepper's* ("Strawberry Fields Forever"), and placed on the album as an afterthought.

Magical Mystery Tour, the British television film, made its debut on December 26. British critics had a field day with their abuse. Such phrases as "The harder they come, the harder they fall," "I cannot ever remember seeing such blatant rubbish," "chaotic," "appalling," and "a colossal conceit" (Schaffner, 90) greeted the Beatles in the morning papers following the preview. Now it seemed that the Beatles were fallible. They had fallen from grace.

Paul McCartney blamed the film's failure on the BBC's decision to broadcast the film in black and white. The Beatles' camp preferred the original color version to the drab black-and-white version. It seemed that the most reasonable explanation for this unexpected failure by the Beatles was the reported drug overdose of manager Brian Epstein on August 27, 1967, who died at the age of thirty-two. Epstein had been the glue that held the now discordant band together. Without him, the group was adrift and headed for destruction. Beatles' fans, however, plodded steadily along in their quest for the truth. What new death clues did this LP hold?

The title song, "Magical Mystery Tour," advised us to "roll up for the mystery tour." What was the mystery? We found that the last line, "The magical mystery tour is dying to take you away, / Dying to take you away, take you today" suggested again that the mystery concerned death. Perhaps the mystery contained more answers to the supposed death of McCartney, and the tour would be a presentation of those clues.

The album jacket contained a photograph of the Beatles dressed in animal costumes. In the center was a black walrus. In certain Scandinavian countries, a walrus is considered a harbinger of death. Immediately, researchers speculated that the McCartney imposter was dressed in the walrus skins.

In *The Beatles Forever*, author Nicolas Schaffner noted that the word *walrus* was derived from Greek, and meant "corpse." Of course, *Webster's Dictionary* lists *walrus* as Scandinavian in origin, not Greek. With this in mind, the public latched on to another clue. It didn't really matter that John Lennon actually claimed that he was the one in the walrus costume, because upon closer examination of the song title, the real truth became evident. The complete title is "I Am the Walrus ('No You're Not!' Said Little Nicola)." Publicly, Lennon claimed to be the walrus, but his own song title refutes this claim. If Lennon was not the corpse, then who was?

In a later Beatles' release, the White Album, Lennon chose to reveal the identity of the walrus corpse in the song "Glass Onion." In the second verse, Lennon sang: " Well here's another clue for you all / The walrus was Paul."

Also on the album cover was a birdlike creature standing over the left shoulder of the black walrus. This birdlike animal wore John's trademark gold-rimmed glasses, thus providing another clue that John certainly was not the walrus!

One of the strangest clues from *Magical Mystery Tour* concerned Ringo's drum head. The drum skin reads "Love the 3 Beatles." Does this suggest that there were only three Beatles left to love? Notice that on pages ten and thirteen of the tour booklet, Paul is standing shoeless, in his socks. As on the *Abbey Road* cover, some fans saw this as another sign of Paul's death since, in some countries, corpses are buried without their shoes. If you look to the left of Ringo's bass drum, you can see Paul's empty shoes smeared with what appears to be blood.

David Sheff's *Playboy Interviews with John Lennon and Yoko Ono* contained John Lennon's take on Paul being the walrus. "When Sheff asked John about the lines "Here's another clue for you all / The walrus was Paul," Lennon stated that the entire lyric was simply a joke and that it really meant nothing. He then explained that the lyric was a simple offering to his long-time friend. John now had Yoko and was leaving Paul.

Later in the same interview, Lennon made additional comments about "Glass Onion." He claimed that the song was merely a "throw away" and that the cryptic line "The walrus was Paul" was only intended to confuse the Beatles' fans. John had also made a comment later that the entire song's lyric purpose was to perplex the intellectuals who sought literary relevance to each new Beatles' lyric. Lennon also stated that the song was only a small piece of poetry and that he could have said "The fox terrier was Paul" (Sheff,177).

After making these comments, Lennon had accomplished his goal: Now, we were all confused! The track "I Am the Walrus" contained more examples of strange clues and bizarre symbols. As previously mentioned, Lennon was greatly influenced by Lewis Carroll, and even received his inspiration for the song from Carroll's "The Walrus and the Carpenter." According to Lennon, "The first line [to "I Am the Walrus"] was written on one acid trip one weekend, the second line on another acid trip the next weekend, and it was filled in after I met Yoko . . . it's from 'The Walrus and the Carpenter.' *Alice in Wonderland*. To me, it was a beautiful poem. It never dawned on me that Lewis Carroll was commenting on the capitalist system. I never went into that bit about what he really meant, like people are doing with the Beatles' work. Later, I went back and looked at it and realized that the walrus was the bad guy in the story and the carpenter was the good guy. I thought, Oh, shit, I picked the wrong guy. I should have said, 'I am the carpenter.' But that wouldn't have been the same, would it?"(Sheff, 164).

As far as being the same, Lennon was probably right. If the song had been entitled "I Am the Carpenter," the religious conservatives would have sworn that Lennon had compared himself to Christ. Surely, John was not ready to start another zealous religious inquisition against himself . . . or was he? On the other hand, Lennon may well have put a great deal of thought into his title. Perhaps he *was* the walrus.

In the poem, the walrus tricks a group of oysters into taking a walk along the beach. The oysters become victims of the walrus's cruel hoax. Was John Lennon making the public his gullible oysters?

One of the most intriguing lyrics in "I Am the Walrus" is the repeated phrase "Goo goo g'joob." This phrase, supposedly taken from James Joyce's *Finnegans Wake*, were the last words spoken by Humpty Dumpty before his famous fall. In a way, it is most appropriate for Humpty Dumpty to be introduced here. Like Paul in the "Paul is dead" theory, Humpty Dumpty also had a tragic accident and cracked his head.

In Lewis Carroll's *Through the Looking Glass*, Humpty Dumpty answers Alice's question, "Must a name mean something?" with the reply, "Of course it must!"

The work presents a series of riddles as Humpty Dumpty attempts to interpret the meaning of Carroll's "Jabberwocky." These references to "Jabberwocky" hint at the same Carollian word play that Lennon enjoyed through his abstract lyrics. These riddles could have inspired Lennon to try the ultimate challenge—placing visual and audio clues that dealt with the mysterious death of one of the Beatles. Lewis Carroll would have been proud!

Lennon and McCartney must have had a great laugh at all the interpretations to the clues, which brings to mind Humpty Dumpty's fractured translation of "Jabberwocky," which led him to think he could "explain all the poems that ever were invented—and a good many that haven't been invented yet." Perhaps Lennon's attempt to baffle and confuse was his way of making the intellectuals who insisted that each Beatles lyric had a complex and hidden meaning look like Humpty Dumpties.

As for Humpty Dumpty's archetypal fall it can be interpreted in a number of ways. First, the fall could have suggested the fall of the Beatles themselves as a group. At this point, the group was no longer the darling of the media. They would be savagely attacked by the critics for their failure in the *Magical Mystery Tour* film. Certain religious groups perceived the Beatles as a threat to the morals of America's youth. Spiro Agnew had led an unsuccessful campaign to remove drug-induced Beatles' songs from the American airwaves. It remained to be seen if the Fab Four would become Milton's Satan and lose Paradise forever. Was it better "to reign in Hell than serve in Heaven"?

Other theories relate the fall directly to McCartney's supposed accident. McCartney is Humpty Dumpty falling off the wall, and "all the king's horses and all the king's men" are the record companies, the production and management firms, and the adoring public who could not bring the real Paul back from the shadowy realms of the dead. The remaining pieces of the band would have to be haphazardly rearranged and a makeshift replacement inserted. This replacement would imitate the true McCartney, in turn keeping the financial empire solvent. It just depended on whether they wanted to play pass the hemlock!

Lastly, the archetypal fall might have suggested the first clues that the Beatles as a whole were on their way to a breakup. As Humpty Dumpty fell and broke into the small fragments that could never again be joined together, perhaps the Beatles, either knowingly or subconsciously, were experiencing their own death throes.

During the making of *Rubber Soul*, tensions among the Beatles grew. Chris Salewicz's *McCartney* cites the following comment from Norman Smith: "With *Rubber Soul*, the clash between John and Paul was becoming obvious. Also, George was having to put up with an awful lot from Paul. We now had the luxury of four-track recording, so George would put his solo on afterward. But as far as Paul was concerned, George could do no right—Paul was absolutely finicky. So what would happen was that on certain songs Paul himself played the solos. I would wonder what the hell was going on, because George would have done two or three takes, and to me they were really quite okay. But Paul would be saying, 'No, no, no!' And he'd start quoting American records, telling him to play exactly as he'd heard on such-and-such a song. So we'd go back from the top, and George would really get into it. Then would come Paul's comment, 'Okay, the first sixteen bars weren't bad, but that middle.' Then Paul would take over and do it himself—he always had a left-handed guitar with him. Subsequently, I discovered that George Harrison had been hating Paul's bloody guts for this, but it didn't show itself . . . mind you, there is no doubt at all that Paul was the main musical force . . . also in terms of production as well. A lot of the time George Martin didn't really have to do the things he did because Paul McCartney was around and could have done them equally well. The only thing he couldn't do was to put symbols to chords; he couldn't write music. But he could most certainly tell an arranger how to do it, just by singing a part—however, he didn't know, of course, whether the strings or brass could play what he wanted. But most of the ideas came from Paul."

On *Sgt. Pepper's* cover, we observed the Beatles dressed in brightly colored band uniforms. Each uniform was of unique and entirely different, vibrant colors. Could this have suggested that the group now considered themselves solely as individuals and not as the similarly clad mop tops from 1964? Perhaps this is why the wax figures are shown gazing down upon a grave.

The Humpty Dumpty clues proved rather interesting, but the first line of "I Am the Walrus" contained a somewhat sinister reference. The lyric stated: "I am he as you are he as you are me and we are all together." This confusing word play contained more Carrollian influences. Lennon had created his own "Jabberwocky," stringing together words that could only be classified as nonsense. But what if the line was interpreted to mean that the unknown "he" was actually Paul McCartney? How could Lennon have possibly been McCartney? And if the mysterious "you" refers to the other Beatles (George and Ringo) how could they also have managed to take the place of their fallen fellow musician and business partner? What if the lines merely suggested that the remaining Beatles would take the place of McCartney in the recording studio? Lennon and Harrison could have played his bass parts; John Lennon could have easily covered the vocals, since it was he who sang most of the songs.

The November 7, 1969, issue of *Life* magazine presented a picture of two sonograms taken by a Dr. Henry M. Truby of the University of Miami. The sonogram of McCartney singing a phrase from "Hey Jude" was suspiciously different from the sonogram containing the phrase "all my troubles" from the earlier recording of "Yesterday." The results? The voices did not match. Could this suggest that there could have been more than one McCartney? Actually, Truby's study stated that there may have been three McCartneys.

Some experts suggested that the sonograms in questions were a closer match to John Lennon. This possible coverup paralleled the lyric from "A Little Help from My Friends." In this case, the Beatles had managed to get by with a little help from their friends. The recordings were made by the band, while the imposter only had to stand and pretend to perform in the Beatles-made films. Incidentally, the BBC banned the promotional film of "Hello Goodbye," because McCartney was lip-syncing his vocal. This violated the rules of the British musicians' union (Dowlding, 190). Obviously, Milli Vanilli was not the first!

"Hello Goodbye" also hinted at a beginning from an end. Could this have been the McCartney imitator who sang, "I don't know why you say goodbye, I say hello"? This might have served as a lyrical clue, sung by the mysterious replacement, William Campbell/Billy Shears, who had luckily stumbled into the role of a lifetime. All he had to do was resemble McCartney, keep the terrible secret, and collect his share of the huge sums of money from the Beatles' royalties.

James Joyce's *Finnegans Wake* also suggested other macabre parallels to the imposter theories. The main character, Tim Finnegan, became drunk and fell from a ladder. Everyone thought that he died from the fall, and his friends held a wake around his body to commemorate his passing. The wake turned into a drunken party ("mirth in funeral") and one of the revelers accidentally poured whisky upon the corpse. Finnegan arose from his coffin and joined in the party. The members of the wake, however, held Tim in his coffin and informed him that an imposter was due to take his place. This imposter, Humphrey Chimpden Earwicker, assumed the role of the good Tim Finnegan. The impostor's initials, H.C.E., were used variously as "Here Comes Everybody." Lennon surely enjoyed such word play. The mysterious H.C.E. was said to have suffered from an obscure disease, perhaps venereal, and he'd peeped at or exposed himself to girls in Phoenix Park. This section of *Finnegans Wake* strongly resembled Lennon's lines from "I Am The Walrus": "Crabalocker fishwife pornographic priestess boy, you been a naughty girl, you let your knickers down." In this phrase we see Lennon's wordplay along with the parallel to Earwicker's exhibitionist feats at Phoenix Park.

Joseph Campbell and Henry Morton Robinson's *A Skeleton Key to Finnegans Wake* suggested that Tim Finnegan was a symbolic reference to the great Irish hero Finn MacCool. In this case MacCool served as an archetype for the mythic, legendary, and religious icons who serve as man's inspiration. These heroes included Prometheus, Osirius, Thor, Christ, and Buddha. The resurrection of the human spirit is shown in the rebirth of Finn as Finn-again which, along with the resurrection of Christ and the regeneration of heroic qualities, brings about hope for mankind.

John Lennon presents further references to Humpty Dumpty throughout "I Am the Walrus" by the Beatles becoming the "eggmen" who represented the cosmic egg of creation itself. The egg symbolically represented "potentiality, the seed of generation, the mystery of life" (Cirlot, 94). The Egyptians believed that the egg contained all that was hidden from mortal man in life, including the occult. "In the Egyptian Ritual, the universe is termed the 'egg conceived in the hour of the Great One of the dual force.' The god Ra is displayed resplendent in his egg. An illustration on a papyrus, in the *Edipus AEgypticus of Kircher* (III, 124) shows the image of an egg floating above a mummy, signifying hope of life hereafter" (Cirlot, 94). This reference to the "eggman" may have represented the cosmic rebirth of the Beatles' essence and an evolution of spirit to an ideal state of wisdom and love.

In *The Lives of John Lennon*, author Albert Goldman states that the mysterious "eggman" was John's nickname for Eric Burdon, lead singer for the Animals. According to Goldman, Burdon was "notorious for cracking eggs on the naked bodies of girls to whom he was making love" (Goldman, 286).

Joyce referred graphically to the members of the wake, the watchers, as they ate everything, including Finnegan's body, which Campbell and Robinson related to the eucharist: "The cosmic egg is shattered but the egg substance is gathered and served for the nutriment of the people, 'sunny side up with care'" (Campbell and Robinson, 5).

The archetypal fall of Humpty Dumpty, the "eggman," relates to this cosmic and metaphysical rebirth. Perhaps the fall is likened to the fall of Adam and man's redemption from original sin, with the end result being the resurrection of hope and the obtaining of the ideal worlds of wisdom and love, with the final defeat and destruction of ignorance and intolerance.

Other passages from *Finnegans Wake* made a case for the elaborate theory of Paul's death. On *Sgt. Pepper's* front cover, the crowd could have been an allusion to the wake. The hand above McCartney's head may have been a symbolic reference to Finnegan's being held in the coffin or, in this case, the decorated grave.

Other lines from the lyric provided further clues to McCartney's tragic doom. Lennon mentioned a "stupid bloody Tuesday," which may have alluded to the night McCartney left Abbey Road studios. Although the fatal accident occurred on a Wednesday morning at five, McCartney supposedly left the studio earlier in the night due to an argument, which would have provided him plenty of time for his rendezvous with destiny.

Lennon also mentioned the phrase "waiting for the van to come," which may have been a reference to the parked van that was involved in the fatal crash of Tara Browne, the Guinness heir, and an allusion to the accident scene in "A Day in the Life." Some observers insisted that the van was actually a reference to an ambulance. This could be correct as the opening musical score was written to simulate the peculiar sound of a British ambulance siren.

Possibly the most fascinating section of "I Am the Walrus" dealt with the obscure, hidden references in the song's long fade-out. Mixed voices that chant "oom pah, oom pah, stick it up your jumpah," and "everybody's got one" along with the droning "goo goo g'joob," are mixed with a frantic orchestral score with cellos and violins ascending and descending in chaotic disorder. Some listeners claim that if the track is reversed the "everybody's got one" becomes "Paul is dead, ha, ha," but, again, this could be another incredible stretch.

At the conclusion, just before the fade-out, actors recite passages from Shakespeare's *King Lear* (4.6.250–60).

> OSWALD: Slave, thou hast slain me: villain, take
>   my purse:
> If ever thou wilt thrive, bury my body:
> And give the letters which thou find'st about me
> to Edmund earl of Gloucester; seek him out
> Upon the British party: O, untimely death!
> EDGAR: I know thee well: a serviceable villain:
> As duteous to the vices of thy mistress
> As badness would desire.
> GLOUCESTER: What, is he dead?
> EDGAR: Sit you down, father, rest you . . .

It is interesting that Lennon chose these lines by accident. According to Lennon, "There was some live BBC radio on one track, y'know. They were reciting Shakespeare or something and I just fed whatever lines were on the radio into the song" (Sheff, 164).

King Lear, considered by many critics to be Shakespeare's masterpiece, is a tale of a foolish king, who unwisely divided his kingdom between his daughters based on his concept of their love for him. Tragically, he found that Cordelia, the youngest daughter, was the most devoted and loved her father through a child's natural duty and not by exaggerated pretense for gain.

King Lear, however, was also a play within a play, and the other story line bore the strongest significance to the quoted lines. The Earl of Gloucester, like Lear, rushed to judgement and, for this rash mistake, suffered greatly. The Earl of Gloucester's crime was being tricked by an imposter. Gloucester's illegitimate son, Edmund, determined to take the inheritance of his half-brother, Edgar, accomplishes this task by interchanging letters. These false letters led to Edgar's disinheritance, and these hidden secrets related to the outcome of the tragic conflicts.

The actors' lines bore a striking resemblance to the McCartney mystery. For example, "Slave, thou hast slain me. Villain, take my purse" may relate to an imposter taking Paul's place following his tragic death. Other bizarre phrases included "bury my body," "oh, untimely death," and "what, is he dead?" Adding these lines of dialogue seemed almost too pertinent to the mystery—something far more than a simple mistake or mere coincidence. Besides, there is another reference to *Lear* in the earlier Beatles' song "Paperback Writer": "It's based on a novel by a man named Lear and I need a break and I wanna be a paperback writer." This substantiated that Lennon and McCartney were well-studied in the tragedy of *King Lear*. (Of course Edward Lear, the English nonsense writer, could explain the Beatles' fascination with off-beat word play.)

The *Magical Mystery Tour* contained other evidence of the fatal end of McCartney. As sleuths pored through the song booklet, careful observers noticed photographs of Paul as cast members posed with their hands raised above the Beatle's head—a death-clue reference that would be repeated in the Beatles' motion picture *Yellow Submarine*. Of course, this animated film also held its share of death clues. In "Only a Northern Song," named after the Beatles' publishing company, George Harrison sings "If you think the harmony / Is a little dark and out of key / You're correct there's nobody there." Earlier in the same song, Harrison sings "When you're listening late at night / You may think the band's not quite right." For some enthusiastic listeners this became yet another reference to Paul's demise. The simple song "Yellow Submarine," during the nautical voice section, supposedly contained John Lennon saying "Paul is dead" followed by "Dead man, dead man." One other strange coincidence occurs during the film, and during the playing of "All You Need Is Love." Some listeners swear that during the song's wind-down they hear John sing "Yes, he's dead" (actually, it's more than likely "Yes, it is"). At this time in the film the word *know* appears on the screen and is transformed to *now*, perhaps suggesting that Paul is dead now.

In one still from *Magical Mystery Tour*, McCartney sits at a desk behind a sign stating "I Was." The British flags behind Paul are crossed in the same pattern used for military funerals. McCartney, of course, is dressed appropriately in a military uniform.

In another still from *Magical Mystery Tour*, the Beatles are dressed in white evening clothes. While John, George, and Ringo wear red carnations in their lapels, McCartney wears a black carnation. Again, McCartney stands out from the others. The black flower was interpreted as a death symbol. In the film production, the Beatles descended a spiral staircase while "Your Mother Should Know" played in the background. McCartney later stated that "I was wearing a black flower because they (the film production crew) ran out of red ones." How lucky that an ordinary black carnation should be backstage! Some investigators insist that if you look closely, the carnations are actually painted upon the Beatles' lapels. If this is true, then someone very close to the film's production made a calculated decision to create the flower mystery. The mysterious flower scene intensified even further, when a young girl appeared and handed McCartney a bouquet of dead flowers. He was the only member of the group to have received such a symbolic gift.

One of the most heavily debated clues was found in *Magical Mystery Tour*'s "Strawberry Fields Forever." Lennon stated: "Strawberry Fields is a Salvation Army home that was near the house I lived in with my auntie in the suburbs. There were two famous houses there. One was owned by Gladstone, which was a reformatory for boys, which I could see out my window. And Strawberry Fields was just around the corner from that. It was an old Victorian house converted for Salvation Army orphans, and as a kid I used to go to their garden parties with my friends. We'd go there and hang out and sell lemonade bottles for a penny and we always had fun at Strawberry Fields. Apparently, it used to be a farm that made strawberries or whatever. I don't know. But I just took the name—it had nothing to do with the Salvation Army" (Sheff, 138).

The audible clue was found near the end of the recording, and came immediately after the music softly faded out, only to slowly reemerge and build once more. Upon careful listening, a faint voice stated something like, "I buried Paul." And thus began the controversy.

David Sheff broached this subject in *Playboy Interviews*.

> SHEFF: What about the line in "I Am the Walrus"
>   [sic]: "I buried Paul?"
> LENNON: I said, "Cranberry sauce." Cranberry
>   sauce is all I said.

The puzzling, unanswered question was that the line did not come from "I Am the Walrus." Actually, the line was from "Strawberry Fields Forever." It seemed unbelievable that Lennon would have mistaken the location of such a controversial lyric.

In *The Beatles in Their Own Words*, McCartney agreed with Lennon's explanation. Paul stated that John's uncontrollable wit led him to shout out phrases on the spur of the moment in the studio. In this case it was "cranberry sauce" and not "I buried Paul." Of course, *The Beatles Anthology 3* collection contained an extremely clear audio track in which the listener can hear John exclaim "cranberry sauce" several times.

Lennon also stuck by his original interpretation in a *Rolling Stone* interview. However, Derek Taylor, one of the Beatles' agents, offered another explanation in a *Life* magazine feature entitled "The Magical McCartney Mystery": "He [Taylor] released a statement from Paul. He [Paul] was, Taylor said, off in the country with his family . . . as for the voice in 'Strawberry Fields,' claims Taylor, it is saying, 'I'm very bored' not 'I buried Paul.' That was as far as Taylor would go. The Beatles didn't expect people to go around reversing their records. He did admit that putting stuff in there in reverse was just the sort of something that sly John Lennon might have done."

It now seemed incredible that both Lennon and McCartney agreed on the hidden message, while Derek Taylor heard a completely different message. The only thing on which all three agreed was that the eerie, softspoken voice did not state "I buried Paul."

John Lennon did manage to spell out his own first name in Morse code. This can be found after Lennon sings: "Let me take you down 'cause I'm going to." At this point, in dots and dashes one can discern J-O-H-N. Obviously, this was an attempt by Lennon to lay claim that this was his song—not just another Lennon and McCartney composition.

If John Lennon had taken the time to place his own name in

a cryptic code, then perhaps a number of the hidden messages concerning the "Paul is dead" rumors may not be as far-fetched as we once thought. Obviously, the Beatles enjoyed throwing in hidden bits of information to tease their fans. It is amazing that, almost thirty years later, most fans are just now becoming aware of the Beatles' incredible senses of humor, and can perhaps listen to Beatle classics with a new regard.

Naturally, some fans wanted to find more exotic clues. If the tape is reversed at the beginning of George Harrison's "Blue Jay Way," a phonetic reversal seems to state "Paul is bloody, Paul is very, very bloody." This section is the reverse of "Please don't be long, please don't you be very long" and, again, this may well be a case of the listener hearing what he or she wants to hear. Actually, George was waiting for his good friend Derek Taylor in a rented house on Blue Jay Way in Los Angeles. If you can hear this hidden message, it may represent the first true phonetic reversal by the Beatles, coming much earlier than the White Album's "Revolution 9."

Another rumor circulating at the time stated that if a sleuth turned the *Magical Mystery Tour* album jacket upside-down and looked at its reflection in a mirror—another similarity to *Through the Looking Glass*—the title, detailed as stars, became the digits to a phone number. The rumor further explained that if the number were dialed, the listener would get the true details of Paul McCartney's death.

In *Shout: The Beatles in Their Generation*, Philip Norman states that the number was actually that of a *Guardian* journalist who was, as would be expected, surprised by a barrage of phone calls.

Theorists determined that in order to properly see the hidden phone number, the large yellow stars in BEATLES must be connected, and then reversed in a mirror. Supposedly, there are

three numbers, depending on whether the album jacket is upside down. Besides the angry *Guardian* journalist, some listeners claimed to have reached a voice that stated "You're getting
closer." Others swear that the phone number belonged to a funeral home, while others claim that the number dialed was answered by a voice belonging to Billy Shears that quizzed them
on Beatles' trivia. Perhaps the callers should have made their
calls on Wednesday morning at five o'clock.

Many believed the mysterious M&D Company, scrawled on
the chalkboard that John Lennon stands next to in the *Magical
Mystery Tour* booklet, may be a funeral parlor. Many followers
of the ironic correctly point out that the caption M, D, and C in
question, which states "The best way to go is by M&D Company," form the initials of Lennon's murderer Mark David
Chapman. This irony, however, tends to be much too disturbing.
Another alarming coincidence deals with the release of the
Magical Mystery Tour LP—December 8, 1967. The album's release date was thirteen years to the day before John Lennon's
murder by Mark David Chapman.

This British import was released shortly before *Sgt. Pepper's*, and, to many fans, the cover contains yet another bass-drum clue to Paul's tragic accident. The shadowy figure's head brings back memories of Robert Freeman's cover photo for *Meet the Beatles* (*With the Beatles*). Notice that the figure's shadowy face is in the same location as Paul's, and, if you look closely, you can see a car that appears to be running off the road into the figure's head.

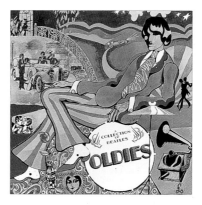

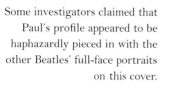

Some investigators claimed that Paul's profile appeared to be haphazardly pieced in with the other Beatles' full-face portraits on this cover.

Some overzealous fans noticed that Paul was portrayed differently from the other members of the group as far back as the *Help* LP; he is the only one not wearing a hat.

Some death-clue advocates claimed that this title may have represented the fatal car accident, and that the Beatles, with somber faces, were looking down into a grave or coffin.

This infamous banned cover demonstrates the Beatles' macabre sense of humor. Not only was it a statement about their concerns about the American packaging of their albums, it also contains some death clues. Note the headless dolls and the false teeth. Remember—it was the Beatles' first actual cover-up!

In this photo, three of the Beatles gather around Paul, who is sitting in an open trunk. Some fans suggested that the death clues originated here. Turned on its side, the open trunk looks like a coffin.

This album cover provided a majority of the clues that led fans to suggest that McCartney had been killed in an automobile accident, and subsequently was replaced by an impostor. Notice the open hand over Paul's head and the waxen images of the Beatles looking down on the grave.

The yellow hyacinth plants appear to spell out "Paul?"

This doll appears to have a toy Aston Martin convertible resting on her right leg. The doll sits on the lap of a stuffed grandmother figure wearing a blood-stained driving glove on her left hand.

The innocent-looking drumskin that we have known and loved for over thirty years contains the most bizarre clue in the "Paul is dead" hysteria.

If you hold a straight-edged mirror perpendicular to the center of "Lonely Hearts," a hidden message appears.

The drumskin, designed by Joe Ephgrave, states, through the mirror's reflection, "I ONE IX HE ◊ DIE." This is a direct reference to the supposed fatal car crash of November 9, 1966 (11/9/66), and the diamond points directly at the victim (McCartney) and at the flower-covered grave where he supposedly now lies.

Paul McCartney wears a black arm band that appears to say "OPD." Many fans interpreted OPD to suggest British police jargon for "Officially Pronounced Dead."

George Harrison points to the opening line from "She's Leaving Home." The lyric states, "Wednesday morning at five o'clock as the day begins." This is another reference to Paul McCartney's accident on November 9, 1966, an accident that reportedly occurred on a Wednesday morning at five o'clock!

Here we have one of the Beatles in the black walrus costume. Notice the gold-rimmed glasses on the figure at the top right. Some researchers believe that by looking at the album cover upside down in a mirror, one can discern a phone number that, when dialed, will explain the truth behind the rumors. (Good luck!)

Blue Jay Way
George Harrison   3:50

Your Mother Should Know
John Lennon-Paul McCartney   2:33

I Am the Walrus
(" *No you're not!* " said Little Nicola)
John Lennon-Paul McCartney   4:35
All side-one selections are
published by Comet Music Corp., ASCAP

...plus these other selections

Little Nicola lets John know that he isn't the walrus.

In this shot from the booklet contained within the *Magical Mystery Tour* album, we see Paul in his socks. If you look to the right of Ringo's drumhead (which reads "LOVE THE 3 BEATLES") you can see an empty pair of shoes that appear to be covered in blood. In this case, as well as in one other photo within the booklet, Paul appears barefoot well over a year before the *Abbey Road* cover.

In the film *Magical Mystery Tour,* Paul, dressed in a military uniform, sits behind a sign that reads "I WAS." The flags are reportedly crossed in the manner of a military funeral.

Three of the Beatles wear red carnations, yet Paul's is black! If you look closely, you can see that the flowers look as if they were painted on the Beatles' lapels. So much for luckily finding one backstage!

In this scene, John stands next to a sign that says, "THE BEST WAY TO GO IS BY M&D COMPANY." The rumor suggested that the M&D Company was a funeral home in Great Britain.

Again, Paul is shown with an open hand over his head—an image that is duplicated on the *Yellow Submarine* cover.

This fishbowl photo does not appear in the film. The rumor is that if you hold the picture at an angle, the lady's beret becomes one of the eye sockets of a skull.

The cover of *The Beatles* (the White Album) seems to be a reference to the traditional color of mourning in some societies.

The BEATLES

This photo of Paul in disguise led many fans to believe that the Beatles had actually included a photo of the impostor, whose name was either Billy Shears or William Campbell.

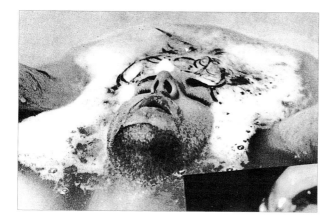

This photo of Paul lying back in the bathtub was said to be
suggestive of a decapitated corpse.

Are these ghostly, skeletal
hands reaching out to
claim Paul?

The four individual photos of the Beatles from the White Album. Notice that Paul's likeness stands out from the other three. Some investigators claim that if you look closely enough, you can see scars (supposedly from plastic surgery) along Paul's upper lip. Was this the result of a motor-bike accident or of a clever attempt to disguise a double?

The alleged funeral procession that started the death-clue hysteria.

The back cover of *Abbey Road* presents a series of dots that appear to form the numeral "3." A crack running through the "S" suggests a flaw within the band. A skull made out of shadow and light ominously seems to follow the Beatles' sign upon the wall.

The *Life* magazine issue of November 7, 1969, was meant to reassure readers that Paul was still with us. Surprisingly, the cover held other clues that added fuel to the death-clue hysteria.

This album, with a cover in funeral black, proved to be the Beatles' swan song. Notice that Paul, again, is presented differently from the others. John, George, and Ringo are in profile with a white background, while Paul faces the camera with a blood-red background.

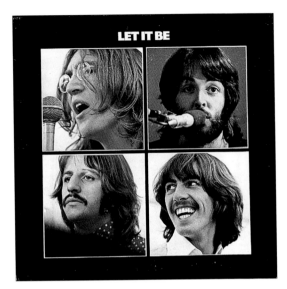

Death rumors were also flying with the release of Paul's solo album, *McCartney.* There is an old English saying, "Life is a bowl of cherries." In this case, the bowl is empty!

CHAPTER 6

The
White
Album

"Here's another clue for you all
The walrus was Paul!"
— *"Glass Onion"*

 For the first time in their careers, the Beatles were convinced that the timing was right to release a double album. This double album represented Paul and John separately, as individuals who performed their songs with the other members filling the roles of back-up musicians. Obviously, it was a turbulent time.

Most of this tension was instigated by John Lennon's intense love affair with Yoko Ono. In his biography, *Lennon*, Ray Coleman revealed that the other Beatles treated Yoko terribly: "John broke a rigid, unwritten rule of the group: that their women would never be allowed in the studios. John perversely attended every session for the White Album with Yoko by his side. His message, unspoken, was obvious to all: they were inseparable. She sat on the speakers, offering suggestions and, incredibly, criticisms."

Bitter arguments soon broke out among George, Ringo, and Paul. At times, Paul appeared to be overly critical of his bandmates' musical contributions. When he criticized Ringo's performance, Ringo left the band. He was gone for a few days, but returned when his bandmates assured him that he was the perfect drummer for the Beatles. George was becoming a much more accomplished songwriter, who now began to resent the Lennon and McCartney song monopoly. Unfortunately, the Beatles, as a unit, continued to grow further apart.

The White Album was released in Great Britain on November 22, 1968, and in the United States on November 25, 1968. The United States advance orders alone numbered 1.9 million copies. By the end of 1970, the album had sold over 6.5 million copies, which made it the best selling double album of all time.

Artist Richard Hamilton formulated the simple cover design for the White Album. The Beatles viewed the artwork as a limited piece of art. The original white cover included the Beatles' name embossed on the front. The later releases simply had the group's name written in light gray. Supposedly, according to Pete Shotton, it was Paul McCartney's idea to have each album individually numbered. There was even a hint that the Beatles had planned a lottery, in which a small number of lucky winners would win tickets to a Beatles' performance in some exotic location.

As magnifying glasses scrutinized every corner and shadow of the Beatle photo foldout, investigators again found pertinent clues to fan the flames of the "Paul is dead" hysteria. The album contained full-face shots of the Beatles individually. Three of the Beatles (John, George, and Ringo) posed similarly. Once again, McCartney's photo was different. Paul's picture was a more detailed closeup than the other three and, under close inspection, it became apparent that there were scars above McCartney's lip—that had not been present in earlier photographs. Could these scars be the aftereffects of the car accident, or the tell-tale signs of plastic surgery? Did this suggest that the Beatles had replaced Paul?

Back in New York City on WABC-AM, Robey Younge was still searching for the answers to the "Paul is dead" rumor. Younge stated in the *Beatle Brunch* interview, "That we went as far as taking accurate photographs and measured the bridge of a person's nose, the 'previous' McCartney and the 'second' McCartney. And it was quite different. One nose was longer than the other. We had experts on. We had a man a doctor [sic] Henry Truby from the University of Miami who specialized in voiceprints. He was the man who used to record baby's cries at birth and twenty years later be able to pick out the individual babies just by their voiceprints. And Dr. Truby told me on tape on television [sic], Rick Shaw and I made a little documentary on it and Truby appeared and said, 'It's definitely not the same person. All my research shows it can't be the same person.' Then we called Dr. Truby to come back and do retakes. He shut up. He clammed up and said, 'No. I can't say anything more about this.'

"When we went to show the tape on the ABC Television Network, we were in New York, in the screening room, just about to get it on that night when a call came from upstairs. 'Cancel it! Don't show it! Don't fool around with it!' Then we let it out to WPIX in New York where they showed it to attorney F. Lee Bailey and he made a copy of it, and he did a pretty good show on it. He interviewed Peter Asher, I told you [Joe Johnson] the story about Peter and his sister Jane. Jane was going to be married to Paul. Well, a friend of mine, Jay Marks, was a broadcaster and a writer for *The Village Voice*. He wrote a book called *Rock and Other Four Letter Words*. After I had done this thing about McCartney, Jay said to me, standing on a street corner in New York, 'I got to tell you Robey. A funny thing, I was at a cocktail party for Paul McCartney and Jane Asher, for their engagement situation. I noticed that Paul was not paying any attention to Jane, but was being rather cozy with Linda Eastman, the photographer girl who had taken the pictures on a recent tour. I asked, 'What is this?' And I was told, 'Don't you know? That's not the boy she fell in love with. That's his replacement. It's all very hush hush you know.' And he [Jay Marks] is not pulling my leg he had credentials [sic]. So there's a bunch of these little things that never came out."

Obviously, some people believed sincerely in the imposter theory. Other photos from the White Album continued to amaze the Beatles' fans.

Another picture of Paul McCartney being pursued by a pair of ghostlike, skeletal hands that seemed to reach out to grab him appeared in the lower right-hand corner of the photo spread containing the song lyrics from the White Album. Could this mean that Paul had fallen victim to the icy coldness of death?

Also included with the album was a fold-out poster that contained several different photos of the Beatles in unusual poses. One photograph showed McCartney in a bathtub with his head underwater, which many investigators believed was another hint at McCartney's alleged decapitation. The British press were similarly shocked when they noticed a picture of McCartney in the nude (behind a cleverly and strategically located white column). Obviously, the Beatles had prepared yet another montage of photographs that many fans claimed laid the foundation for even more cryptic clues.

As usual, most emphasis centered around the songs and the song lyrics themselves. In the song "Glass Onion" the lyric "Here's another clue for you all / The walrus was Paul" could have meant that the hoaxer was Paul. Remember, it was the Walrus who misled the oysters: 'O Oysters, come and walk with us!' / The Walrus did beseech. / 'A pleasant walk, a pleasant talk, along the briny beach: We cannot do with more than four, to give an hand to each'" (Carroll, *Through the Looking Glass*). In this case, if the Walrus were Paul, it only stood to reason that the carpenter was Lennon. Together, they could have deceived the gullible press and public, who heard what they wanted to hear and saw what they wanted to see.

This explanation would give John the chance to symbolically and indirectly represent Christ as the carpenter. During the making of "Revolution 9," John Lennon announced to his friend Pete Shotton that he (Lennon) was actually Jesus Christ. This occurred near dawn during an LSD trip. Lennon then called the other Beatles, as well as business associates at Apple, and immediately broke the news to them. The stunned neodisciples were shocked, and perhaps a little irate, about being disturbed from their sleep by such a revelation. They announced that they needed more time to consider this oracle.

Lennon appeared to be sincere in this belief. However, Christ allusions aside, the carpenter's task has always been to construct, and perhaps John was carpenterlike in his creation and building of one of the greatest hoaxes ever perpetrated on the public. Did we, like the foolish oysters, accept this bizarre premise blindly? Where was the concrete evidence that common sense demanded? Wasn't it time for the cold, hard facts? And where was the body anyway?

The reference to Lewis Carroll's conversation between the Walrus and the oysters ("we cannot do with more than four") may have intricately related to the four Beatles' albums under discussion: *Sgt. Pepper's*, *Magical Mystery Tour*, the White Album, and *Abbey Road*. These four albums contained the bulk of the death clues under scrutiny. Perhaps Lennon was telling us, in his Carollian way, that these albums, like oysters, had to be opened and examined closely to find what pearls of wisdom the Beatles had placed to enlighten their fans.

"Glass Onion" also contained references to other Beatles' songs, convincing many fans that these songs contained other clues to Paul's death. In the first verse, Lennon sings: "I told you about Strawberry Fields / You know the place where nothing is real." To many listeners, the phrase "Strawberry Fields Forever" was reminiscent of the eerie phrase "I buried Paul."

The line "nothing is real" refers to the Beatles' movie promo of "Strawberry Fields Forever." In the promo, when the line "nothing is real" is first mentioned, Paul's face appears, suggesting that this is not the face of the real McCartney.

Lennon also sings "Looking through the bent backed tulips / To see how the other half live." Did the bent backed tulips represent the flowers around the drum skin on *Sgt. Pepper's* cover? Did "to see how the other half live" suggest the mysterious lookalike—the other half of Paul McCartney? Perhaps the other half referred to a reflection of reality, the alterego of Paul McCartney—William Campbell or Billy Shears. Also, in the song "Lady Madonna," the "Wednesday morning papers didn't come." To some, this may have hinted at a news blackout that hid the tragic consequences from an unknowing world the morning that Paul was said to have died. Even the phrase "Glass Onion" may suggest looking at the *Sgt. Pepper's* drum skin through a looking glass, in the sense that both an onion and a drum have a skin.

John sings that he is also "fixing a hole in the ocean." I'm sure that many fans remembered the strange "Be At Leso" clue and were convinced that John was referring once again to Paul's watery grave.

Ringo Starr also contributed a song to the White Album. The song "Don't Pass Me By" actually reached the number-one position in Scandinavia. Many sleuths heard evidence of the tragic automobile crash in the song's last verse when Ringo sang: "You were in a car crash and you lost your hair." The car crash in which the victim lost his hair reinforced the decapitation theory. Mentioning the terms "doubting" and "unfair" might have suggested tension that arose among the Beatles—specifically between Paul and Ringo. The reference to being late, "about an hour or two," could have suggested the original theory that McCartney left Abbey Road studios angrily on a "stupid bloody Tuesday" and "blew his mind out in a car." All of this was said to have occurred on November 9, 1966.

Perhaps the most haunting song on the White Album was "While My Guitar Gently Weeps," by George Harrison. The strange imagery of a bluesy guitar that wept in somber, melodic strains was compelling. The line "I look at the world and I notice its turning" could have simply meant that life continued. In this case, the Beatles struggled onward as a group following the tragic death of one of its members. At the conclusion of the song, many sleuths heard Harrison's softly moaning voice exclaim "Paul, Paul," sadly during the song's fadeout. This longing voice could well have convinced some listeners that this was yet another clue to McCartney's death, as a distraught George Harrison remembered his fallen partner.

The Beatles were pioneers when it came to avant-garde experiments with previously untried recording techniques. The Beatles, for instance, were the first group to record backward passages in their music. John, in particular, was adamant about the use of backward tracks. The public today is only too aware of supposed backward masking techniques. The religious right has held countless seminars to acquaint today's youth with hidden Satanic messages. Led Zeppelin's "Stairway to Heaven" has always been popular airwave fare on dark and gloomy Halloween nights, as disc jockeys across the country astonish their listeners by playing the hidden message "My sweet Satan." It is debatable whether there are secret, dark, and mysterious messages on certain albums. Some rock groups actually increased their record sales when they denied the hidden messages contained in their recordings.

There are a number of critics who also claimed that the Beatles were influenced by Satanism. After all, Aleister Crowley, The Great Beast, was included on *Sgt. Pepper's* album cover. Allegedly, the Mark of the Beast (666), written in red, appeared upon Crowley's forehead upon close examination. The use of Satanic symbolism perhaps reminded critics of the archetype of the devil's sacrifice—the death of a member of a coven in exchange for wealth and success. This theory may have suggested that the Beatles offered McCartney in a sacrificial rite for fame and fortune, as the Rolling Stones were said to have offered up Brian Jones. As a further coincidence, one Rolling Stones album was entitled *Their Satanic Majesties Request*. What could have been this macabre request?

Many believers were sure that Satan's request was the blood of Brian Jones. Tragedy has always seemed to stalk rock-and-roll bands. For instance, the untimely, tragic deaths of Bon Scot of AC/DC, Duane Allman of the Allman Brothers Band, Randy Rhodes from Ozzy Osborne's band, Keith Moon of the Who, Jimi Hendrix, Janis Joplin, Jim Morrison, and Kurt Cobain, as well as countless others, fit this description. It seems that rock and roll has its own recurring ghost stories, so much the better for modern legends.

The first backward vocal track performed by the Beatles was in the song "Rain." Lennon had always stated that the Beatles were the first band to pioneer the use of backward recording methods. For instance, John claimed that while playing one of the early renditions of "Rain" through his home-stereo head-phones, he somehow inadvertently reversed the tape. The swirling cacophony led him in, suggesting that his vocal fade-out be played in reverse and mixed into the final recording. The hidden message? John, however, merely repeated the first vocal line from the first verse of "Rain," "If the rain comes they run and hide their heads."

When questioned about Lennon's new-found love of back-ward recording techniques, Beatles' producer George Martin also commented upon the Beatles' curiosity that led them to create new textures and sounds that led to even greater self-expression. Another use of a Beatles' reversed recording was Ringo's backward cymbals on "Strawberry Fields Forever." Martin explained that in time the Beatles grew tired of this technique and moved on to experiment with other sounds and developed newer recording procedures.

Once the thrill of backward tracking became commonplace, the Beatles utilized this technique as a vehicle for disguising death clues within their songs. The first instance is found just after "I'm So Tired" and just before "Blackbird." It seemed ap-propriate that this message appeared in this particular location since a blackbird (raven) in literature has always served as a symbol of approaching death. For example, in Shakespeare's *Macbeth*, Lady Macbeth referred to a raven that signaled the ap-proach of King Duncan. Edgar Allan Poe's "The Raven" forced the poet to contemplate the eternity of death "that will be lifted nevermore."

Coincidentally, perhaps, there are several Poe references in Beatles' history. First, a gloomy Edgar Allan Poe stood among the crowd on *Sgt. Pepper's* album jacket. In "I Am the Walrus," John Lennon sang, "Man you should have seen them kicking Edgar Allan Poe."

Poe wrote a series of columns dealing with the solution of secret ciphers for a Philadelphia newspaper, *Alexander's Weekly Messenger.* As Poe's fame grew, so did his reading public. Possibly his greatest cryptic work was called "The Gold-Bug," which contained secret messages that had to be decoded by his readers. Poe's motifs centered around the themes of living burial and the return from the dead. This concept played nicely with the Beatles' mystery and *Sgt. Pepper's* album cover, which depicted a staged funeral that may have been premature. Was Paul like Ligeia and destined to return from the dead in another body—that of an imposter? Or could the Beatles' conspiracy have referred to the first great detective story, Poe's "The Purloined Letter"? In this work, the clues were in front of the police at all times; nothing was hidden. The answer to the mystery could only be solved through careful deduction and close observation. Wouldn't it be just as proper for the Beatles to scatter their albums with mysterious clues, and place them directly under the noses, and ears, of the public where they have been virtually unnoticed for over thirty years? What inspiration! Poe, as well as Lewis Carroll, who also delighted in designing puzzles and mysteries, would indeed have approved of such clever deception. The Beatles, through modern-day recordings, were able to produce many more cryptic sensory clues than Poe and Carroll's jumbled visual symbols.

The hidden backward message followed "I'm So Tired," with John Lennon singing: "I'd give you everything I've got for a little peace of mind." The strange murmuring sounds are faint, and obviously recorded backwards. According to Mark Lewisohn's *The Beatles: Recording Sessions*, Lennon, when questioned about these strange mutterings, actually said he had whispered, "Monsieur, Monsieur, how about another one?" After countless listenings, it remained doubtful that this was the actual message. However, when the track was reversed, it sounded like: "Paul is dead now, miss him, miss him, miss him." This mysterious voice softly uttered Paul's melancholy obituary. Other listeners claim that the voice says, "Paul is dead man, miss him, miss him, miss him."

Though this reversed message was indeed bizarre, it was nothing compared to the chilling revelations of "Revolution 9," which, ironically, would be voted the most unpopular Beatles' track in a poll by *The Village Voice*. George Harrison confided that he hardly ever listened to it. George Martin, along with Paul and Ringo, tried to keep the song off the White Album. Lennon had a different opinion; he enthusiastically declared it "the music of the future."

As the recording started, the test engineer dutifully and monotonously repeated, "Number nine, number nine" over and over again, thirteen times, until the voice faded out into a void of sounds. Symbolically, the clue had to do with the number nine. Could the nine possibly be related to the mysterious date of the accident—November ninth? Perhaps the clue had to do instead with the singling out of the victim. By counting the letters of the Beatles' last names, sleuths discovered that Starr contained five letters (Starkey had seven letters), Lennon was made up of six letters, Harrison possessed eight characters, but only McCartney fit the correct pattern with exactly nine letters. Was this yet another attempt to identify the corpse?

Lennon's references to the "Number 9" became an obsession with him. The numeral played a pivotal role in his life and began with his birth on October 9, 1940 at 6:30 P.M., until his untimely death on December 8, 1980 at 11:07 P.M. Eerily, both 6:30 P.M. and 11:07 P.M. add up to nine. If you take into consideration the five-hour time difference between England and New York John Lennon's death would have been officially announced on December 9, 1980 in Great Britain.

The Beatles were first discovered by Brian Epstein on November 9, 1961. What may be relevant, however, was that November ninth could have represented the hidden message on the *Sgt. Pepper's* drum skin. In this case, the mandala had been completed. If the grave represented a death occurring on that particular date, then the Beatles would have come full circle with their symbolic deaths as a band occurring exactly on the fifth anniversary of their discovery by Epstein. It would be grand if the Beatles followed in the steps of William Shakespeare, another English master lyricist, and died on their birthday. The release of *Sgt. Pepper's* could very well have signaled not only the symbolic death of the group, but a rebirth of four unique individuals who now had very little in common, but nonetheless worked diligently until they developed their own different musical styles. The Beatles would have achieved what Carl Jung referred to as "the ultimate state of oneness." This symbolic circle could be related to the *Yin-Yang principle*—the ever present mixture of light and darkness, and masculine and feminine traits, that denoted the cosmic energies of the universe (Cirlot, 47-8).

The duality of November 9, 1966, was another strange coincidence. Paul's supposedly fatal accident occurred on the same date that John Lennon met Yoko Ono. This was ironic, since Yoko Ono is often blamed for the Beatles' breakup. In this case, the drum epitaph was actually precognition—the exact prediction of the beginning of the Beatles' death throes!

There are other views on the number nine symbol. According to G. A. Gaskell's *Dictionary of All Scripture and Myths*, the number nine in Far Eastern Indian symbolism "relates to the number three, the number of perfection and completeness. Nine, which is of course three squared, refers to the attainment of perfection on the three lower planes." Obviously, as far as a rock-and-roll band goes, the Beatles had reached this perfection.

In *A Dictionary of Symbols*, Cirlot noted that the number nine is "the end-limit of the numeral series before its return to unity. For the Hebrews it was a symbol of truth, being characterized by the fact that, when multiplied, it reproduces itself . . . In medicinal rites, it is the symbolic number par excellence, for it represents triple synthesis, that is, the deposition on each plane of the corporal, the intellectual, and the spiritual."

This Far Eastern concept of death and rebirth also related to "Niflheim, the shadowy region of death—the ninth world. The object of existence is the formation and growth of the soul which is immortal while its lower vehicles are subject to decay and extinction while the soul is being purified stage by stage. The purified souls of individualities shall rise from the lower planes by the unpurified personalities and shall continue to reincarnate below until they are perfected" (Gaskell, 535). This could possibly apply to the reincarnation of the Beatles as a new group, with a new identity, as well as the new musical direction, which was certainly evident since *Sgt. Pepper's*.

The strange case of "Revolution 9," which credited Paul McCartney as co-writer, began with the test engineer's droning voice repeating "Number nine, number nine, number nine." As the narration continued, other discordant sounds—radio broadcasts, sirens, applause, gunshots, sports cheers, the sound of crackling fire, screams, a baby gurgling, a choir singing, and other unidentifiable sounds—are introduced into the melange.

The structure of "Revolution 9" began with the long fadeout track of the Beatles' "Revolution 1." This provided the basic

rhythm for the track. Then, a series of taped recordings rang-
ing from classical music and standard sound effects were cut
into varying lengths, thrown up into the air, and reassembled
piecemeal into a bizarre montage of sounds. Ten tape machines
were used to play back the newly created montage as it was re-
recorded over the basic "Revolution" track.

In listening to "Revolution 9," we first hear a series of spoken, almost whispered, conversations. Possibly the first recog-
nizable pattern is where a voice can be heard saying, "Every one
of them knew that as time went by they'd get a little bit older
and a little bit slower." (This occurs a little over a minute into
the basic track.) Another understandable phrase is identified as
"Who could tell what he was saying? His voice was low . . ."

A spooky backward track also appears when a man's voice
screams over and over again, "Let me out!" "Let me out!" This
follows what appears to be the sounds of a terrible collision and
the sounds of crackling flames. To many Beatles' fans, these obscure sounds represent a recreation of Paul's terrible accident.

Other questionable reversals are said to include phrases
suggesting "She used to be assistant," or "There were two men."
Of course, some active imaginations suggested that the second
phrase was actually "There were two now they're gone." Was
this a reference to Paul and Rita?

The most interesting tape reversal from "Revolution 9" was
found in the reversal of the test engineer's "Number 9 . . . Number 9 . . . Number 9." Though the reversal is somewhat slurred,
listeners can make out a plausible "Turn me on dead man" (or
"Turn me on dead mun"). To make this explanation fit sleuths
claimed that we had to take into consideration their British ac-
cent; therefore, "dead man" becomes "dead mun." Like many
backward tracks dealing with phonetic reversals, many experts
consider this to be coincidental.

At the conclusion of the track, a voice can be heard saying "A fine natural imbalance ... must have got it between the shoulder blades ... The Watusi ... The Twist ... Eldorado." The best way to hear the hidden messages is to turn down the left stereo channel, and listen to the track only through the right channel.

One true hidden track can easily be found in "Revolution 9." About five minutes into the track, just after the sounds of an applauding crowd, blaring sirens, and the sound of what appears to be a ticking stopwatch, a voice states something like "So the wife called, and we better go see a surgeon . . . so any and all, he went to see the dentist instead, who gave him a pair of teeth, which wasn't any good at all."

Life magazine's "Magical McCartney Mystery" contained a further transcription. The article went into great detail concerning the backward sounds of the car crash, and the voice screaming "Let me out." The line "so the wife called, and we better go see a surgeon," is identified in the article as being "He hit a pole! We better get him to see a surgeon." *Life* also mentions a series of phrases that include: "My wings are broken and so is my hair" (maybe a reference to Ringo's "Don't Pass Me By": "You were in a car crash and you lost your hair"); "I'm not in the mood for words" (was this an attempt to show the surviving Beatles mourning over a departed member?); and "Find the night watchman. A fine natural imbalance. Must have got it between the shoulder blades" (perhaps other allusions to a police coverup and the fatal injuries).

As the reader must surely now be aware, not everyone heard the same message, but there are some phrases that seemed to be agreed upon. This may have provided further evidence that we heard what we wanted to hear, and that our imaginations had to fill in the pieces of the mysterious puzzle. Many researchers interpreted "So the wife called and we better go see a surgeon" as "So, all right, Paul, then we had better go and see a surgeon."

The backward track of "Let Me Out" occurs between tape-counter positions 058 and 062. Perhaps the strangest occurrence is when a voice states at 6:43 seconds into the track, "Take this brother, may it serve you well." Was this another attempt at providing more fuel to the already blazing funeral pyre of Paul McCartney?

The reference to "Turn me on, dead man" may have been a reference to Lennon's earlier statement concerning the writing of "A Day in the Life." According to Lennon, "Paul's contribution was the beautiful little lick in the song, 'I'd love to turn you on,' that he'd had floating around in his head and couldn't use" (Sheff, 164). Could this be another hint that this line was another attempt at identifying the dead man as Paul McCartney?

CHAPTER 7

Charles Manson's "Helter Skelter," the Beatles, and the Strange Case of William Campbell

Not surprisingly, more than death-clue advocates were influenced by the White Album. Charles Manson, who had established himself as Jesus Christ incarnate to his believing family, also developed a theory concerning the symbolic meaning of the White Album. Manson believed that the Beatles were actually angels sent by God to reveal the secrets of the terrible approaching apocalypse. This apocalypse, foretold in the Biblical book of Revelation (the New Testament book of prophecy), was interpreted by the Manson family to suggest the Beatle song "Revolution 9." Since "Revolution 9" contained such horrible and bizarre sounds, the family was convinced that the recording was actually the sounds of Armageddon itself.

In the Manson family belief, "Revolution 9" referred to Revelation, chapter 9. In this Biblical book, four angels would be loosed from the Euphrates River to summon the destruction of man: "And the four angels were loosed, which were prepared for an hour, and a day, and a month, and a year, for to slay the third part of men."

Manson believed that this Armageddon would involve a racial war between whites and blacks, and that the Beatles were the four angels prophesied to start the last days of man in the years of the great tribulation. This racial war was proclaimed "Helter Skelter." John Lennon stated that he had nothing to do with Manson's misconceptions of Beatles' lyrics. Somehow, Manson's beliefs were centered around George Harrison's song about pigs ("Piggies") and McCartney's fond remembrances of an amusement park slide that he named "Helter Skelter," hardly the stuff that would foretell Armageddon.

According to Manson, blacks, led by the Black Panthers, would arise and slaughter the white "piggies." George Harrison offered an explanation of his song "Piggies." Harrison claimed that the song was merely a social commentary, and the line "All they need is a damn good whacking" was suggested by his mother to complete the rhyme. It "had absolutely nothing to do with American policemen or California shagnasties!"

According to Charles Manson, there were still other references cleverly hidden throughout the White Album. There was the mention in "Honey Pie" that "my position is tragic / Come and show me the magic of your Hollywood song." Manson believed that the Beatles wanted and needed his influence and involvement to help fulfill the deadly prophecy of "Helter Skelter." He was to provide the direction through his magical "Holly-wood Song." Later, in the same song, the Beatles continue with "Oh honey pie you are driving me frantic / Sail across the Atlantic / To be where you belong." The lyric also mentions "I'm in love but I'm lazy" which Manson interpreted as meaning that he must make the first contact and lead the world to the brink of the apocalypse. Apparently, on many occasions, Manson and his family members unsuccessfully placed phone calls to the Beatles' management trying to make contact with the four "angels of revelation." In "Don't Pass Me By," "Blue Jay Way," and "Yer Blues," the Beatles constantly mention waiting for someone to arrive. Charles Manson thought this to be himself, the incarnation of Jesus Christ. To him, it was the ultimate invitation to become the fifth Beatle as well as the fifth angel, to complete the ninth chapter of "Revelation": "And the fifth angel sounded and I saw a star fall from Heaven unto the earth; and to him was given the key of the bottomless pit . . . and they had a king over them, which is the angel of the bottomless pit, whose name in the Hebrew tongue is Abaddon but in the Greek tongue hath his name Apollyon." It was extremely clear to each of Manson's followers that Abaddon and Apollyon were effective aliases for Charlie.

The Manson family had planned to survive the apocalyptic holocaust by hiding out in the desert until the racial war was completed. In the lyrics of "Helter Skelter," the Beatles sing "When I get to the bottom I go back to the top of the slide / Where I stop and I turn and I go for a ride." Manson interpreted this as his followers emerging from the bottomless pit. The family would arm themselves with machine guns and convert stolen jeeps into dune buggies. The Mason family would then rise up and forcibly seize power from blacks. Charles Manson would then rule supreme in his new utopia on earth. For instance, the lyrics to "Revolution 1" state "But when you talk about destruction / Don't you know that you can count me out." (Here a voice saying "in" immediately after the last word "out" can be heard.) The Beatles also mentioned that they would "like to see the plan," which Manson again interpreted as an invitation to provide the Beatles with his plan for "Helter Skelter."

Charles Manson was convinced that his plan would be in

the form of an album that he would record, with the complete approval of the Beatles, to help show the world the "magic of his Hollywood song." Manson interpreted the lyrics to "I Will" as evidence to back his plan: "And when at last I find you / Your song will fill the air." He also noticed that at the conclusion of "Piggies" there are a number of oinking sounds followed by the sounds of machine-gun fire. This had to be the start of the racial apocalypse.

Manson was a charismatic figure. One popular urban legend stated that he, like Stephen Stills of Crosby, Stills and Nash, was said to have auditioned for a role in a new television production that parodied the Beatles. This new television program was to be called *The Monkees*. Stills was rejected because of his bad teeth. Manson possibly was refused for his strange, seemingly psychopathic, behavior. Perhaps his grubby appearance did not maximize his chances either. Of course, as is the case with many urban legends, this incredible story is considered to be pure myth.

In *Heroes and Villains*, Steven Gaines tells how Manson, once befriended by Dennis Wilson of the Beach Boys, used this connection to take advantage of Wilson's property and connections. It even seemed that the Beach Boys recorded one of Manson's songs, "Cease to Exist," without Manson's knowledge. This almost prophetic title was changed by the Beach Boys to "Never Learn Not to Love." This song, included on the *20/20* album, was the B-side to the album's first release, "Bluebirds over the Mountain."

Manson was furious that his lyrics had been changed, and that his song had been readapted to the Beach Boys style. His anger was also directed toward record producer Terry Melcher, Doris Day's son, whom Manson believed had wrongly denied him a recording contract. It was this catalyst that prompted the family to choose the residents of 10050 Cielo Drive as victims. It didn't matter that Melcher no longer lived in this house. The new resident was Sharon Tate, pregnant wife of film director Roman Polanski. Her house guests included Jay Sebring, her former boyfriend and popular hairstylist; Abigail Folger, heiress to the Folger coffee fortune; and Voytek Frykowski, Folger's boyfriend. Their innocent deaths provided a chilling warning to Terry Melcher, and was a barbaric massacre that sickened the world.

When the police entered the Tate home, they found the four savagely mutilated bodies and noticed that the walls were covered in slogans written in the victims' own blood. These slogans read "Helter Skelter," "Political Piggy," and "Arise."

The slogan "Helter Skelter" referred to Manson's concept of the approaching racial war which would lead to Armageddon. The phrase "Political Piggy" bore reference to the victims of such a race war. The last word, *arise*, also referred to the upcoming racial war. It seemed that in "Blackbird" (a song Manson believed symbolically stood for the black race, especially the Black Panthers) McCartney sang: "You were only waiting for this moment to arise." This lyric is repeated over and over throughout the song. Manson believed that blacks had to be shown the method in which to begin the great apocalypse. They would have to "take these broken wings and learn to fly."

The family committed the murders, and led the way to revolution as they demonstrated the proper method for slaughtering the white "piggies." One of the murderers, Susan Atkins, was given the nickname "Sexy Sadie." Perhaps the Manson case served as the ultimate warning for those fans who suffered from acute Beatlemania. It was not always harmless to interpret lyrical meanings. In this case, someone's interpretation proved deadly, and provided chills to those listening to hidden messages. The boogie man had now come out of the darkness.

After the White Album was released, Paul McCartney envisioned a live Beatles' concert. It was time to take the Beatles back on the road and play before their devoted fans. Apple's Derek Taylor went as far as to promise that there would be a concert. However, the friction between the group continued, and Paul reminded the other members that they had been in a period of mourning for Brian Epstein. The essential spark provided by Epstein had always been discipline. At first, the Beatles naturally rebelled against it, but now they had to pick themselves up and promote their own discipline that would allow them to continue as a group. It appeared that the Beatles had become a ship adrift.

Obviously, McCartney was ready to assume the mantle of leadership of the band but, in this regard, he found only resentment. Harrison was much more content in maintaining the unstructured studio environment in which the Beatles' songs could be polished until perfection. A live appearance was way too risky, and would only lead to bickering between the band's members and a forced compromise. The final studio results would showcase the Beatles' music without flaw.

Paul and musical director Michael Lindsay-Hogg suggested staging this new concert either at an ancient coliseum in Tunisia ("You know it's just impractical to try and get all these people and equipment there," said Harrison) or on a ship in the ocean (Harrison: "Very expensive and insane . . . I don't think you're going to get a perfect acoustic place by the water out of doors"). Lennon offered his own suggestion: "I'm warming to the idea of an asylum" (Schaffner, 117).

When news of this dissension reached the press, the concert was canceled, and fifty lucky winners who were supposed to receive tickets to the Beatles' concerts received free Beatles' albums instead.

The Beatles placed a great deal of pressure on themselves. What direction remained unexplored? Could the band ever produce a revolutionary musical synthesis to rival their own *Sgt. Pepper's?* The public expected just that. *The Beatle Monthly,* a publication dedicated to news of the Beatles, ran a column by S. C. Blake who, speaking for many of the Beatles' fans, demanded that the Beatles continue experimenting with new sounds, look into the future, and lead their art form into even greater inventiveness. He criticized any attempt by the Beatles to rediscover their musical roots as "going backward into Rock and Roll! A run-of-the-mill sound of three guitars and a drum kit."

The Beatles had indeed looked to the future. Other changes helped distance the group from themselves as well as from their adoring public. John Lennon and his wife Cynthia were divorced and Lennon married Yoko Ono. John believed that marriage was not necessary but that a "happening" could result from their marriage. John's experimentation with the avant garde continued with his recordings made with Yoko. Long tracks of her screaming vocals accompanied only by John's electric guitar feeding back in equally frenzied tones led *Rolling Stone* to suggest that the new sounds were "like a severely retarded child being tortured."

John experimented with his own backing group, which he called the Plastic Ono Band, and recorded the politically relevant "Give Peace A Chance." The Lennons staged bed-ins, hair peace, took out billboard ads that stated "War is over if you want it—John and Yoko," and suggested that each world leader be given acorns to plant to grow the seeds of world peace.

John wrote "The Ballad of John and Yoko" which commemorated John and Yoko's social revolution. This song was rushed into production, with only John and Paul performing on the track. The song did not receive extensive radio play in the

United States, however, since the chorus included the refrain, "Christ, you know it ain't easy." This phrase reminded American disc jockeys of Lennon's earlier remarks about Christ. Of course, with Brian Epstein now dead, John repeated his original comment concerning Christ. He stated that he was "Christ's biggest fan," and that, "Yes, I still think it. Kids are more influenced by us than by Jesus" (Schaffner, 122).

This strange behavior only alienated John further from the group, and created a puzzle for his old, unchanging fans. George Harrison immersed himself in Far Eastern musical forms and recorded songs dealing with his involvement with Hare Krishna. He also released a solo album entitled *Electronic Sound*. According to one music critic, the solo offerings of Lennon and Harrison were "unfit for human ears."

Ringo became more interested in the acting profession, and landed a movie role in Terry Southern's *Candy*. He also was involved with Peter Sellers in *The Magic Christian*. Of course, John Lennon had maintained that Ringo was the best actor of all. These dramatic changes now pulled the Beatles in their separate directions, but the unthinkable was yet to happen. Stranger than the death clues that shook the media was the startling revelation that, on March 12, 1969, Paul McCartney married Linda Eastman. Young women throughout the world mourned his passing from bachelorhood. Now, all the Beatles were married.

Paul's marriage was not wholly unexpected, but everyone was sure that the lucky girl would be his long-time love and fiancée, Jane Asher. As the death clues surfaced, many fans pointed to this marriage as proof that this McCartney was truly an imposter. The rumors suggested that the McCartney lookalike, William Campbell, or Billy Shears, married the girl of his own choice and that the remaining members of the Beatles paid a huge cash settlement to a heartbroken Jane Asher, ensuring her silence concerning the death of the real McCartney.

Linda Eastman was a successful photographer, whose pictures of the Beatles and other rock bands appeared throughout rock-music fan magazines. McCartney, the family man, secluded himself from the crowds and recorded his first solo album, *McCartney*.

Although these solo projects were being carried out by the Beatles as individuals, the group was busy recording songs for *Let It Be*. This album was postponed and later produced by Phil Spector, but it was a departure from the famous Beatles' sound. For the first time in the group's history, female backing voices were used on Beatles' tracks. Paul McCartney was furious with the overproduction of "The Long and Winding Road," which he had considered another "Yesterday." This only served to increase the tremendous strain among the members.

The Beatles brought along a movie crew to film the recording of the *Let It Be* soundtrack. The mounting tension was evident everywhere. George Martin described the turbulent recording sessions as bordering on chaos. Since Paul tried to maintain the proper discipline necessary to complete the project, the other members considered him overly bossy. Band members would take days off from the sessions, and John was constantly concentrating his attention to Yoko. The result was a general disintegration.

George Harrison recalled starting the *Let It Be* sessions in a happy frame of mind. He had just returned from the United States, where he enjoyed the freedom and cooperation of American musicians. He soon found that things at the Abbey Road studios were back to normal. He felt that Paul had always maintained a superior attitude over him musically, and had neglected including a number of Harrison's compositions on past Beatles' albums. Watching the *Let It Be* film, the tension is extremely obvious between Paul and George.

Harrison, in a February 1977 *Crawdaddy* interview, added: "There's a scene where Paul and I are having an argument. . . . and we're trying to cover it up. Then the next scene I'm not there, and Yoko's just screaming, doing her screeching number. Well, that's where I'd left and I went home and wrote "Wah-Wah." It'd given me a wah-wah [headache], like I had such a headache with that whole argument, it was just a headache." George's "Wah-wah / You've given me a wah-wah" later appeared on his album *All Things Must Pass*.

There is a bitter irony to the Beatles' *Let It Be* film. In some ways it paralleled the making of the *Magical Mystery Tour* television special. The Beatles' idea behind the *Magical Mystery Tour* was to bring a camera and just film what happened along the way. Unfortunately, nothing happened. The concept behind *Let It Be* was to preserve a filmed record of the Beatles' legacy and creativity within the recording studio. Sadly, what resulted was the complete record of the deterioration of the world's most popular band.

Most of us could not imagine what pulled the Beatles so far apart, but the answer was not terribly hard to comprehend. It was mainly financial. The Beatles' Apple Corps Productions lost great sums of money. Lennon complained that the Beatles faced certain bankruptcy. Since Epstein's death, the Beatles' fortunes had been dwindling. There were too many people on the Beatles' payroll, but the group could not come to an agreement on who their new business manager should be.

At this stage, Allen Klein came into the Beatles' lives.

Klein, a successful businessman, especially appealed to John Lennon. Perhaps this was due to Klein's early life, which resembled that of Lennon. Lennon commented that in a number of ways Klein was very much like him. John was also impressed that Allen Klein knew his work and understood his lyrics. The single most compelling factor in Lennon's allegiance to Klein was in the manager's understanding of the complex relationships within the Beatles. In John's words, "He knew every damn thing about us."

John, Ringo, and George were determined that Klein should handle their business affairs, while Paul insisted that his new father-in-law, Lee Eastman, be the new business manager. The Beatles' wars continued. The financial rewards for this position were overwhelming. Brian Epstein had received 25 percent of all total Beatles' funds. The right man could easily make millions of dollars.

Klein ruled Apple. He cut everything that was not indispensable. Paul McCartney and John Lennon were influenced to write "You Never Give Me Your Money," in honor of the financial crisis. (This song, released on the *Abbey Road* album, was also rumored to have a cryptic death clue. One line states, "One, two, three, four, five, six, seven, all good children go to Heaven." Was this another reference to Paul being in the afterlife? Another coincidence occurs when the single digits are added together. The result is twenty-eight, the same numeral that appears on the Volkswagen's licence plate, hinting at McCartney's age at his supposed death.) Allen Klein, however, managed at least one financial plum—he negotiated with EMI records for an increased royalty rate of sixty-nine cents per album. This rate was unheard of at the time, and raised the retail cost of an American album to seven dollars (Schaffner, 123).

This may have helped win Paul over to Klein's side, as the financial situation improved somewhat, but the tension between band members remained. One day in 1969, John Lennon visited Paul McCartney and informed him that it was over, and that he wanted a divorce. John no longer wanted to be a Beatle.

CHAPTER 8

The
Abbey
Road
Clues

"One and one and one
Is three."
— *"Come Together"*

 Since the material for the *Let It Be* album sat unused in the studio, the Beatles made plans for what proved to be their last recording session. Paul McCartney approached George Martin, and asked if they could make an album like they had in the past. Martin remembered being surprised at Paul's offer, but agreed as long as the members would allow him to produce the album in his way with their complete confidence in his direction.

Under the guidance of George Martin, *Abbey Road* was recorded quickly and brought back memories of the early excitement the Beatles generated in the pre–*Sgt. Pepper's* recordings. Though the magic still lingered, so did the stress that finally ripped the Beatles apart.

The conflict grew between the members of the group, but now was much more noticeable between Lennon and McCartney. It seemed that *Abbey Road* would be split between the primitive rock-and-roll songs of John Lennon and the lush, heavily produced numbers of Paul McCartney. Martin enjoyed working with Paul in developing a pop, orchestral antithesis to John's raw, creative energy. Actually, *Abbey Road* became yet another compromise that the Beatles knew only too well. John Lennon was given the first side to showcase his songs, whereas Paul's delicate interweaving of melodies comprised the album's second side and reflected the creative partnership between George Martin and Paul McCartney.

McCartney recalled the tensions behind the sessions in an April 16, 1971 *Life* magazine article. He and John were now openly critical of each others' musical directions. Paul felt that John was now only interested in performing his own compositions. Reflecting again on the sessions in an October 1986 issue of *Musician*, McCartney, in hindsight, considers himself to be just a little too bossy or "producery" for the other members. It appeared that the other members constantly reminded him of his actions and frankly told him "to piss off!" At this point, Paul realized that he had become overbearing, and immediately kept his opinions to himself. After all, George Martin was the album's producer. However, after the sessions began to drag and become sterile after a few days Ringo turned to Paul and said, "Come on . . . produce!" At this time, the other members, perhaps reluctantly, fully realized Paul McCartney's combined role as writer, musician, and, now, producer.

The tension between John and Paul continued to escalate. One night, during the recording of *Abbey Road*, Paul called in and announced that he would be missing the session in order to celebrate the anniversary of his meeting Linda. The couple had planned a romantic evening together. Lennon became furious. He arrived at Paul's home at 7 Cavendish Avenue, screaming at Paul for inconveniencing the other members. The episode ended when John smashed one of his original paintings that he had given to Paul.

Abbey Road also contained a single that was released only to bring in money for Apple Productions. This was done at the insistence of Allen Klein and, surprisingly, the A-side of the single belonged to George Harrison's "Something." Lennon later referred to this composition as the best recording on the album. Frank Sinatra went even further, exclaiming that "Something" was "the greatest love song of the past fifty years."

The song proved so popular that it was used as a TV commercial for Chrysler LeBaron Coupes in late 1987 and early 1988. This was about the same time that Nike reportedly paid Capitol Records $250,000 to use the Beatles' version of "Revolution" in their TV shoe ads. This concept of commercialization was met with mixed opinions. Yoko Ono believed that Nike should use the Beatles' version, and that "John's songs should not be part of a cult of glorified martyrdom. They should be enjoyed by kids today."

McCartney stated, "I haven't made up my mind . . . generally, I don't like it, particularly with the Beatles' stuff. When twenty more years have passed, maybe we'll move into the realm where it's okay to do it."

The release of *Abbey Road* took place on September 26, 1969, in the United Kingdom, and on October 1, 1969, in the United States. In the United States, the recording entered the album charts at number 178, jumped to number four within the first week, and reached number one the following week, where it remained for eleven weeks. It stayed in the top thirty for thirty-one weeks. The total world sales were estimated to be 10 million at the end of 1980.

Of all the Beatle albums that generated the McCartney death clues, *Abbey Road* proved to be the most sinister. The album jacket contained a photograph taken at Abbey Road at ten in the morning on August 8, 1969. In *John Lennon: One Day at a Time*, Anthony Fawcett shared this story behind the album cover's photographs. Paul McCartney had arrived without his shoes, and everyone thought it quite amusing. Obviously, his house was just around the corner, but he decided that he would be fine in the photo shoot as he was. Ian McMillan, the photographer, had set his camera up in the center of Abbey Road just outside the studio entrance. The police stopped traffic as the Beatles walked in single file across the now-famous crosswalk. The walk was performed three or four times, as McMillan would shout out directions until he was satisfied with the results.

After completing the front cover, McMillan and Fawcett drove along Abbey Road searching for just the right street sign to photograph for the album's back cover. McMillan wanted one of the older, tiled signs set into the worn brick wall. When the proper sign was found, the camera was set up, and a series of shots were taken. According to Fawcett, McMillan became quite angry when a girl wearing a blue dress just happened to walk by, ruining one of his photographs. When the photos were developed, the Beatles chose this same shot of a mysterious girl in a blue dress as the back-cover photo. It seemed Paul McCartney took a very active role in choosing this particular photograph, and called it the most interesting of the completed photos.

The album photographs meant much more to the legions of Beatles' mystery sleuths, who searched painstakingly for clues to McCartney's death. The four Beatles walking precisely across the street was thought to have symbolized a funeral procession. Since John Lennon was dressed completely in white, he was said to have represented the church, or even the deity—

white, of course, being the traditional color of mourning in many Eastern cultures. Ringo, who was next in the procession and dressed neatly in black, represented the undertaker or, better yet, the priest who respectfully followed Lennon's deity. Paul McCartney followed Ringo, and was barefoot, with his eyes closed. In a number of societies, corpses are buried without their shoes. Again, many assumed that this figure was the great Beatle imposter.

This Paul held a cigarette (a coffin nail) in his right hand, when every true Beatles' fan knew that the real McCartney was left-handed! The McCartney look-alike was also out of step with the other three Beatles. John, Ringo, and George were in perfect step. Each led with his left foot, while McCartney led with his right.

McCartney remembered the photo scene in a *Rolling Stone* interview in 1973. The shoeless Beatle commented that it was a nice hot day in London, and that he just didn't feel like wearing his shoes. He also commented that this innocent photograph "turns out to be some old Mafia sign of death or something."

This simple explanation would be very convincing if it weren't for the fact that on the *Magical Mystery Tour* cover Paul appears in two other scenes barefoot. In one scene, his empty shoes stand next to Ringo's drum kit, and appear to be covered in blood. George Harrison, dressed in work clothes, was the last of the group in the procession and, to many, represented the gravedigger.

Equally puzzling is Paul McCartney's explanation for why he chose not to wear shoes: "a hot day in London." Everyone knows that, on hot days, asphalt becomes unbearably hot. Surely, then, McCartney would have realized his dilemma when faced with the photograph session and the infamous walk across Abbey Road.

One of the most puzzling things about this scene is why the Beatles chose to walk across the street from west to east. Since there are song references to the sun on *Abbey Road* ("Here Comes The Sun" and "Sun King"), the Beatles may have been referring to the sun's cycle and related this to a comparison of the human lifespan. In ancient societies, in Egypt in particular, the dead were buried facing west. In Egypt, early Pharaohs were enshrined in their houses of eternity on the western side of the Nile. This would be in accordance with the cycle of the sun as it sets in the west. Of course, it is traditional in Christian societies for corpses to be buried facing east. This represented the glorious rising of the dead that followed the teachings of the Christian rapture. If the Beatles symbolically represented a burial scene, it would seem logical that the group should walk from east to west, and represent the earthly cycle of birth to death. The visual clues now suggested that the album photograph did not represent a burial but, instead, a resurrection, since the band was walking counter to the sun's path to the east, in this case, denoting a new birth. This followed the Eastern concept of the rebirth of Krishna, which generated this new era of wisdom and love.

The reference to the Beatles' song "Sun King" may also have brought back memories of the French absolute monarch, Louis XIV. Louis was known as the Sun King and became one of the most powerful and feared monarchs throughout Europe. As a bizarre afterthought, in Alexander Dumas' novel, *The Man in the Iron Mask*, the Sun King is replaced by his imposter twin brother, whose face had been hidden behind an iron mask. Was this yet another reference to the imposter theory?

If one looked over the inside shoulder of George Harrison, an eerie message is shown on the license plate of the parked

Volkswagen Beetle. The license plate reads "LMW 28IF." The "28IF" represented the age of the true Paul McCartney. In this case, McCartney would have been twenty-eight were he alive. It didn't seem to make much difference that Paul was actually twenty-seven years of age when *Abbey Road* was released.

The cynics countered that in far Eastern societies an individual's birth included the time spent in the mother's womb. In this case, Paul McCartney would indeed have been twenty-eight. According to McCartney, in a February 1988, *Musician* interview: "That Volkswagen has just recently been sold for a fortune. But it meant nothing you know."

Actually, according to Mark Lewisohn's *The Beatles: Recording Sessions* the Volkswagen sold for over 2,300 pounds at a Sotheby's auction in 1986. Louis Yager actually placed a phone call to the owner of the Volkswagen. He accomplished this by going through automobile registration records and placing an overseas call to a London number, rather late one night, awakening an elderly lady who simply and mysteriously "declined comment" (*Life*, November 7, 1969).

It would be in dramatic, grim irony to have a Volkswagen Beetle serve as conclusion to the tombstone introduced on the *Sgt. Pepper's* drum head. In this case, the age of the deceased Beetle, or Beatle, now completed the full epitaph. With the drum-skin message, we learn who died and the date of the death. The Volkswagen gives us the age of the individual, and helped complete the cycle that began with *Sgt. Pepper's*.

On the back side of the *Abbey Road* album cover is Fawcett's grimly shadowed stone wall. The picture contained a montage of light and shadow. A sign that reads *Beatles* is displayed prominently against the wall in large block letters. Each letter was perfectly formed, except for the letter *S*. There is a small, jagged crack, running through the imperfect letter. This possibly hinted at a flaw within what was once thought to be the perfect rock-and-roll band.

Examples of these imperfections included the hand over McCartney's head and his back turned to the camera from *Sgt. Pepper's Lonely Hearts Club Band;* Paul dressed in military dress and the black carnation he wore from *Magical Mystery Tour;* Paul's closeup photograph from the White Album; and the mysterious funeral procession for *Abbey Road.*

The back of *Abbey Road* contained other death clues. To the immediate left of *Beatles* etched into stone, a series of dots appear to be machine-gunned haphazardly against the wall. If the dots are connected in the fashion of the popular children's game, Connect the Dots, one can easily make out the number three. After the number three becomes visible, the complete sign would then read "3 Beatles." However, everyone knew that there were four Beatles, and that, on the front of *Abbey Road,* the four members were pictured walking across the street. What if the clue meant that, of the four, only three were original members? One, then, must surely be a replacement or imposter. This fit perfectly with the "Paul is dead" hysteria.

One of the most intriguing questions concerned the girl in the blue dress who just happened to pass by at the time of the photograph. Many investigators concluded that the girl was none other than Jane Asher, the one-time fiancée of McCartney. Of course, this could be another example of a fertile imagination at work, but Jane Asher was a model, and a great number of Beatles' fans, at this time, refused to accept Paul's marriage to Linda Eastman.

In the recordings on *Abbey Road,* there are also clues that reinforced the death theory. The first song of side one is a John Lennon rocker, entitled "Come Together."

The lyric content of "Come Together" contained some allusions that helped convince Beatles' listeners that tragedy was hidden beneath the lyrics. The first verse started with a reference to "flat top," which many sleuths suggested was a reference to a headless body or a victim of a severe head injury. The same verse mentioned that the mysterious "he" had "hair down to his knee." John Lennon was into Hair Peace and Bagism, as evidenced in the line "Bag production," but, again, many observers interpreted this line as a reference to the fact that, in death, a corpse's hair continues to grow. The last line of the first verse mentioned a reference to a joker who simply does what he pleases. This line strongly hinted at the idea of a hoax. Was McCartney the joker who did as he pleased? In this case, could Paul have managed to pull off the greatest hoax in music history? The line "He wear no shoes shine" may refer to the barefoot McCartney walking across the cover of *Abbey Road*.

There are other examples of standard Beatles' humor on the album. "I Want You (She's so Heavy)" ended abruptly in midbar progression, and the second side of *Abbey Road* ended with a tongue-in-check composition, entitled "Her Majesty," which was not mentioned on the playlist.

The "Come Together" chorus suggested another return to the *Sgt. Pepper's* album cover. Again, the observer is reminded of the wake scene in which "a crowd of people stood and stared" at the flower-decorated grave of the fallen Beatle. Were these people, as well as the surviving members of the Beatles, coming together as mourners at the funeral service? The phrase "over me" perhaps referred to the corpse that rested peacefully in his grave, as the onlookers paid their last respects by gazing at his casket.

Later, in the third verse, another allusion to the walrus is given. Possibly the most intriguing line was found in the fourth verse. The phrase "He say one and one and one is three" referred to the back side of the *Abbey Road* album cover, and brought to mind the mysterious dots that, when connected, formed the number three; in this case, another reference to the number three, or the three surviving Beatles.

The next line suggests that perhaps Paul, "the cute Beatle," may very well have been too hard to see in the shadowy netherworld of death.

CHAPTER 9

Number Nine?
Turn Me On,
Dead Man!

THE *LIFE* MAGAZINE ARTICLE OF
NOVEMBER 7, 1969, AND
PAUL'S REPLY

"Number nine?
Number nine?"
—*"Revolution 9"*

When radio station WKNR-FM lit up the airwaves with the grim news of the death rumors in October 1969, the public demanded to know the truth: If Paul McCartney were not dead, then where was he? The other Beatles refused to comment, except for Ringo who called the rumors "a load of old crap." Ringo related that John Lennon was dressed in the black walrus suit on the cover of *Magical Mystery Tour*—not Paul McCartney.

The rumors continued. To get to the bottom of the mystery, *Life* magazine sent a group of reporters to find Paul McCartney. Press agent Derek Taylor had given the press an official statement claiming that Paul was not dead, but only in Scotland. At this time, the reporters were determined to bring back a scoop. The small group, cameras in hand, made their way to the McCartney residence. Angry at the invasion of his family's privacy, McCartney tossed a pail of water over one of the photographers. Ironically, the McCartney residence was outside the

Scottish town of Campbelltown. (William Campbell?) In a matter of minutes, Paul had regained his composure and made his way into town to apologize for his unseemly behavior. Ever wary of the public's perception, Paul offered the photographers exclusive Linda McCartney photographs of himself and his newborn infant. He was also to have stated, like Mark Twain, "Rumors of my death have been greatly exaggerated. However, if I was dead, I'm sure I'd be the last to know."

Life magazine's London correspondent Dorothy Bacon ran an exclusive interview with Paul McCartney concerning the "Paul is dead" rumors in the magazine's November 7, 1969 issue. In the interview, McCartney offered a number of explanations for the mysterious clues. First, he claimed that the OPD arm patch he wore on the *Sgt. Pepper's* cover actually stood for "The Ontario Police Department" and that he picked it up in Canada (actually the patch contained the letters OPP); the black carnation he wore in *Magical Mystery Tour* was simply due to the fact that the production company had run out of red ones. Paul claimed that John was dressed in black on the cover of the *Magical Mystery Tour* album (in this case he agrees with Ringo); as far as being barefoot, McCartney claims that he was barefoot only because it was a hot day. As for being picked out as the focal point of the rumor, he merely suggested that he had not been in the news lately and that he enjoyed his privacy. He ended the interview by stating that the "Beatle thing" was over and that any comments from him would come in his songs.

McCartney recalled later, in a radio interview, that someone at Apple asked what they were to do when American disc jockeys spread the word of Paul's tragic accident. McCartney replied, "Sounds like good publicity to me. Tell them I'm not." Of course, this response took weeks to reach the media. This gave the public plenty of time to buy Beatles' albums, and search for even more clues.

In a radio interview from Chicago in 1980, furnished to me by my friend Jay Fox from the ABC Radio Network, McCartney gave this puzzling account that contradicted many of his original explanations for the earlier phenomena. The interviewer starts by asking "Were you the walrus?" And Paul responded that he was still the walrus. He claimed that this was just a "much read-into thing" and that in the making of the *Magical Mystery Tour* album he just happened to pick up the walrus head and became the walrus for the photo. It meant nothing. It was also just a joke that he had turned his back on the *Sgt. Pepper's* cover. In at least one other interview, Paul was said to have been in the walrus suit because he was the only one who could fit into it. Strangely enough, in the 1969 *Life* magazine article, Paul stated rather forcefully that it was "John in black" on the cover of *Magical Mystery Tour*. Accordingly, these contradictions add to the perpetuation of the death-hoax mythology.

Almost incredibly, the photo of McCartney accompanying the *Life* magazine article suggested yet another clue to Paul's demise. The back of the magazine cover, which depicted McCartney and his family with the glad tidings that "Paul Is Still with Us," contained an advertisement for an automobile. If the cover photograph is held up to the light, the automobile is seen across McCartney's chest blocking out his body. Paul's head is the only discernible image that breaks through the black void. This is yet another eerie coincidence pointing toward McCartney's having been decapitated in an automobile accident.

The Beatles, as a group, ebbed slowly following the release of *Abbey Road*. The long-awaited Phil Spector production of *Let It Be* was finally ready for release, and now served as the grand finale for the world's greatest rock-and-roll band. Unfortunately, the Beatles still squabbled over which should be released first: *Let It Be* or Paul McCartney's solo album, simply titled *McCartney*. Paul refused to allow his album to wait until after the *Let It Be* release. With the purpose of changing Paul's mind, Ringo was sent by the others to help solve the release problem.

In Peter McCabe and Robert D. Schonfeld's *Apple to the Core*, the authors presented Ringo's account of the visit. Ringo stated that when Paul heard that the other Beatles had suggested he put off his solo album release date, McCartney simply exploded. He hurled threats claiming that he would "Finish you all now" and that "You'll pay!" After seeing the importance of the solo project, Ringo suggested that he and his bandmates let McCartney have his way.

McCartney did indeed have his way, and *McCartney* was released in April 1970. To many investigators, even this solo LP held a death clue. The cover depicted an empty bowl of cherries. Could this refer to the saying, "Life is a bowl of cherries"? Only, in this case, the bowl was empty!

Along with this release, Paul made it official that he was no longer a Beatle. McCartney's surprise announcement infuriated John Lennon. Lennon felt that he should have left the group earlier, and that Paul had managed to trick him into staying a Beatle much longer than he had originally wanted. John referred to the making of *Let It Be* as "hell . . . it was the most miserable session on earth" (*Rolling Stone*, September 11, 1986).

George Harrison's comments echoed Lennon's statement: "I couldn't stand it! I decided, this is it! It's just not fun anymore; as a matter of fact, it's very unhappy being in this band at all" (Dowlding, 256).

Paul, however, went for the jugular. At his press conference, his official statement stated that his break from the Beatles was "due to personal differences, musical differences, business differences, but most of all because I have a better time with my family" (Schaffner, 135). Contained within the *McCartney* solo album was a series of questions and responses that approximated a staged press conference. Paul took this opportunity to include a few more digs at his bandmates. Paul stated that he had no desire to be another John and Yoko, and when asked if during the making of the *McCartney* solo album he had missed working with his old friends and bandmates or perhaps the creative suggestions of producer George Martin, McCartney coldly countered with a resounding "No!"

It now appeared that the *Let It Be* LP design was perfect: funeral black. The color may not have only insinuated Paul's death, but also served as the obituary for the Fab Four. Other death clues from *Let It Be* included Paul's looking directly into the camera lens, while the other Beatles present their left profiles.

Each of the three Beatles in profile have a white background, whereas McCartney's background is blood red! In December 1969, *The Beatles Monthly* (the major fan magazine for the Beatles) ended after seventy-seven issues. The magazine had been in existence before the release of "She Loves You." In parting, the fan magazine took these shots at the individual Beatle members: "The Beatles were denounced for having grown uncooperative about posing for photographs; for having failed to come out against drugs; for having lost their sense of humor ('Everything seems to be very, very serious. Nothing is just plain fun anymore'); and even for their appearance ('The Beatles are certainly tremendously photogenic, or at least they were in the days when you could see all of their faces')" (Schaffner, 131).

The Beatles now pursued solo careers, but were not always as successful as they might have imagined. Ringo released *Sen-*

timental Journey (originally entitled *Ringo Stardust*) in 1970, and dedicated it to his mother. The selections included "Love Is a Many-Splendored Thing" and showcased the big-band era. The critical reaction to this album was simply embarrassed silence. Ringo later went to Nashville, Tennessee, and recorded his *Beaucoup of Blues* LP with Pete Drake and other Nashville session players. It was obvious that the former Beatle had a fondness for country music (e.g., "Act Naturally").

When the single "Back Off Boogaloo" was released in March, 1972, the normally calm and peaceful Ringo lashed out at a mysterious meathead in these lines: "Wake up meathead, don't forget that you were dead." Was this meathead Paul McCartney? Was this an attempt to confirm the public's suspicions of the great death hoax? Ringo, John, and George often used the code name "Boogaloo" to secretly refer to McCartney. In one instance, Starr remarked that he had "Boogaloo on the phone."

It seemed appropriate that Ringo released *It Don't Come Easy* earlier in 1971, and that this effort, for once, towered above Lennon's *Power to the People*, McCartney's *Another Day*, and Harrison's *Bangla Desh*. It seemed that Ringo stood out from his more prolific songwriting partners and was finally allowed his place in the spotlight.

John Lennon released his signature album, *Imagine*, in October 1971. The album contained "How Do You Sleep?" an attack on Paul McCartney. In a caustic putdown of his long-time partner Lennon sang, "Those freaks was right when they said you was dead." With this lyric, Lennon acknowledged the American rumors that Paul was dead. Some later critics claim that Lennon referred only to McCartney's decline as a writer. Lennon also parodied the McCartney *Ram* album by enclosing a postcard showing himself posing with a pig. John peered mischievously into the camera, and there could be no denying the object of John Lennon's scorn.

Although George Harrison did not attack McCartney directly at this time (he would later attack both Lennon and McCartney), he did take part in the production of both songs. He played the guitar lines for each composition and joined in as a fellow conspirator.

The search for an explanation to the death clues continued. The Beatles only stated that there was no attempt on their part to mislead the public. In the *Playboy Interviews* (1980), David Sheff asked Lennon if he was amused by the rumors of Paul's death and the hysteria it inspired. John responded, "They all had a good time. It was meaningless" (Sheff, 81).

From a *Rolling Stone* interview dated January 7, 1971, the interviewer asked John if any of the clues were purposely placed on the albums. Lennon replied that the whole thing was made up. He did recall one earlier instance when the Beatles playfully placed the phrase "tit tit tit" in "Girl," however. John was also asked about the "Paul is dead" rumors while he and Yoko were guests on the Dick Cavett show in 1970. A member of the television audience asked, "Last year we had a big thing about Paul McCartney being dead. And I was wondering how much of it was planned and how much was planned by you?" John answered, "It had nothing to do with me. . . . There is a rumor that he is dead actually, but the first I heard about it was in the press you know. I don't know how it happened. It was a mystery to Paul. It was a mystery to me. None of us knew what it was about or whatever. But of course they credited it to me or Paul saying, you know, that it was publicity seeking and we did it. It was too far-out for us to have thought of it, you know. And it wasn't a very, I don't know. It was a peculiar thing. I don't know what it was about."

In an unreleased John Lennon interview with Dan Chandler in London 1971, provided to me by my friend Joe Johnson of *Beatle Brunch,* Lennon claimed that when he first heard the rumors he laughed. However, they got more and more serious. He said that he had no idea how it got off the road and he was sure that many people believed it to be one of Lennon's publicity stunts or put-ons. Strangely, he claimed that if he had thought of it he may have put it in, but the whole thing was totally beyond belief. After a short pause he compared it to the controversy surrounding his infamous quote concerning Christ and Christianity, and that perhaps some disk jockey wanted to start a scene.

Despite Lennon's public denial of the rumors, the conspiracy theories of Paul's death continued to grow. Joel Glazier, an early proponet of the "Paul is dead" conspiracy, would set up booths at Beatle conventions and present the clues to the fans. Joel went further than the simple death clues however; his scenarios included a belief that the CIA was responsible for Paul's death in order to end the Beatles' influence over the younger generation. This same theory has recently been used to draw John Lennon's assassination into the covert wing of the CIA. Still another of Glazier's plots dealt with some ritualistic, occult conspiracy to sacrifice members of famous bands in order for the group to maintain its popularity and keep up its record sales at any cost.

In the early days of the death rumors, Lewis Yager called Alex Bennett's talk show and "claimed to have been awakened in the night by the screams of a Beatlemaniacal girlfriend to whom McCartney's dire fate had been revealed in a dream." Yager later made this statement: "Everyone knows it was a hoax. But people still love hearing the clues. It was the most fascinating stunt in years."

Sociologist Barbara Suczek, in her essay "The Curious Death of Paul McCartney," interviewed typical thirteen- and fourteen-year-olds and recorded their feelings that related to the death clues. The typical responses told of cold and creepy feelings that were, at times, depressing. In short, much the same way you felt when you first heard the clues or held that small, straight-edged mirror to the center of the Lonely Hearts Club Band drum from *Sgt. Pepper's* cover.

It seemed that grim irony continued to follow the Beatles after their breakup. The senseless murder of John Lennon on December 8, 1980, in New York City, brought back memories of previously released Beatle material, such as the album *Revolver* (John was killed with a handgun), and the Beatles' song "Happiness Is a Warm Gun," which many investigators believed hinted at Lennon's possible use of heroin.

The most bizarre reference to John's death is contained in the opening lyric line to "Come Together." John's vocal muttering exclaimed "Shoot me." "Me" is hidden behind the first notes of the bass-guitar line.

In another bizarre twist, John and Yoko lived in the Dakota apartment complex in New York, which served as the site for Roman Polanski's *Rosemary's Baby*, a film based upon Satanism and the occult. Strangely, during the *Playboy Interviews*, John heard a scream from outside and stated, "Oh, another murder at rue Dakota (laughter)" (Sheff, 91). The list of Lennon coincidences helped provide a chilling retrospect to the "Paul is dead" rumors.

The field of psychology also became extremely interested in the McCartney death rumors. A 1976 tome, titled *Rumor and Gossip: The Social Psychology of Hearsay*, by Ralph Rosnow and Gary Fine, featured an extensive passage on the McCartney hoax, which the authors also explored in the August 1974 issue of *Human Behavior.* The two psychologists concluded that, like most rumors, this one was spread as an unconscious attempt on the part of rumor mongers to gain status in exchange for precious information. In this regard, the spreading of the "Paul is dead" rumors resembles that of the ever-popular collections of urban legends.

Another prevalent theme addressed in the article was the credibility gap between the people and the American government, especially the Lyndon Johnson presidency and the Spiro Agnew resignation. It appeared that answers were being withheld concerning domestic issues, as well as the Vietnam War. Add to this mistrust the Warren Commission report and the many rumors that surrounded the Martin Luther King and Robert Kennedy assassinations, and we have a generation fostered on conspiracy. It was possible for many people to believe that a famous figure could be secretly replaced for three years without anyone finding out. We lived in a world dominated by *Mission Impossible* and, in that age, anything was possible and probable.

The human race, it seems, has always been obsessed with the macabre. Stephen King's novels take us by the hand and lead us into the darkest recesses of our hidden fears. Of course, we have to look into the void. We cannot hide our eyes, cry under the covers, and scream for our mother's assurance that it is only a dream. In this case, we, as a species, are fascinated by our own mortality.

The creepy and tingly feelings described by the fourteen-year-olds in Barbara Suczek's study confirmed that we all have primeval fears that have existed since the dawn of time. In 1945, a series of rumors concerning the death of Franklin Delano Roosevelt swept the nation: "Newspapers, radio stations, banks, and even corner drugstores were deluged with calls asking if it were true that this, that, or the other person had died, or been killed in an accident" (Jacobson, 460).

While theories of hidden conspiracy and intrigue have been proven for the most part to be groundless, there is still that remote chance that a researcher may stumble upon the one elusive gem of wisdom that will bring forth new evidence, solve the hidden mysteries of the past, and lead the way to a better understanding of those significant figures who helped shape our history, our culture, and our very lives.

Throughout our literary history, man has written tales of heroes and gods. In certain instances, heroes are reborn to be worshiped as gods, as in the case of Alexander the Great. This premise may have been the catalyst behind the entire Beatles' death theory. The rumors became elements of the traditional epic. The *scops* (storytellers) were the rumor seekers who sang their songs to the mesmerized multitudes. The clues were passed down by word of mouth to preserve the lifeline between fact and legend.

In "The Curious Case of the Death of Paul McCartney," sociologist Barbara Suczek lists five specific points dealing with an explanation of the McCartney mystery and how the cryptic clues ascended to the realm of legend.

In the first case, new learners were instructed by the masters, those who knew the clues, as to the proper meaning and interpretation of the death clues. Only one interpretation seemed justified. Any other explanation was frowned upon, and the only proper explanation was passed down to each new convert. In many ways, this would resemble the passing down of doctrine through a Masonic rite, or in the granting of the mystic goodies during a fraternity initiation. Another parallel to the fraternal investiture is the fact that it is done verbally, from one member to another.

Second, the life or death of the legendary figure becomes ir-relevant. The general public may become confused as to the ac-tual existence of the figure, and accepts the information willingly. In this manner, the legend becomes symbolic of man and his institutions, therefore, the passing of the rumor does not require confirmation to sustain it.

Third, the twin pillars of death and the occult provide for the general acceptance of the myth. From Norse, Greek, and Roman mythology, the hero has to overcome supernatural forces and death to achieve his destiny.

Fourth, the accepted myth involves the premature death of a youth who is transformed by death into a god. This is a preva-lent theme from Osiris and Achilles to Jesus Christ. The pattern of birth, death, and rebirth has long been a teaching of both pa-gan religions and Christianity. Perhaps this theme has always appealed to man to give him hope that he, like the great epic he-roes, can overcome death through his unswerving faith or by reincarnation.

The last element of the myth lies with its entertainment value. As the ancient rhapsodies used suspense to make sure their audiences returned, so did the tellers of the "Paul is dead" myth. The story was so chilling that the probability of repeat-ing the clues one by one was extremely high. In this case, the legend perpetuated itself through a willing audience eager to extend the doctrine of a new myth.

The so-called McCartney myth relates to one of the more memorable legends in English literature, that of the Fisher King. According to Gertrude Jobes' *Dictionary of Mythology, Folklore, and Symbols*, the Fisher King is the archetype for a "king whose virility is tied to the fertility of the land." If the king be-comes ill, impotent, or wounded, his lands begin to wither and die. The old king finds comfort through fishing, thus the title

Fisher King, and can only be restored by a seeker of the Grail. At this time, the king is healed and his lands are restored.

The Grail is a literary, as well as Christian, symbol that relates to the cup that Christ drank from at the Last Supper. The same cup, according to legend, was used by Joseph of Arimathea to collect Christ's spilled blood during the Crucifixion. The quest for this miraculous cup has been a source of inspiration from Sir Thomas Mallory's *Le Morte d'Arthur* to Steven Spielberg's *Indiana Jones and the Last Crusade*.

The Beatles themselves could have filled the symbolic role of the Fisher King. In 1967, Lennon was convinced that the older Beatles' material had become a "wasteland" of thought. With this in mind, the Beatles opened new dimensions in thought and sound, with the introduction of *Sgt. Pepper's Lonely Hearts Club Band*. The public readily accepted the new sounds and musical direction of the Beatles vision. However, the creative period of *Sgt. Pepper's* was short lived. The Beatles once again sank into the dismal wasteland of disillusionment. The group argued amongst themselves. Their music became sterile, and the band broke up.

The radical sounds of "Revolution 9" served as an attempt to lead the rock visionaries into even more unexplored realms of sound. As the Beatles withdrew from the public eye, the magical world of rock and roll became unfruitful. The cryptic clues associated with the album covers and song lyrics became the challenge for a new quest—a quest that would return the creative sounds to the long silent songsmiths. Perhaps the music world is waiting for the seeker of the Grail who will once again lead them into yet another golden Renaissance of sound.

Unfortunately, in today's musical marketplace, most groups are prepared to look the same and sound the same. There is no deviation from what have become the accepted norms of appearance and performance, so the land grows barren and waits for the new possessor of the magical sounds that will free yet another generation from complacent mediocrity.

The Fisher King symbol is apparent on the *Sergeant Pepper's Lonely Hearts Club Band* cover. The cycle of birth, death, and rebirth is evidenced through visual clues. The waxwork figures of the Beatles represent the birth of the band. The members are posed in look-alike outfits and stand above their own grave. The symbolic death of the Beatles is portrayed by the freshly dug grave, complete with the floral arrangements. The rebirth symbol is found in the *Sgt. Pepper's* era—Beatles dressed in their psychedelic finery. The Beatles had now become the beautiful butterflies, released from the imprisoning cocoon of social mores. The birth, death, and rebirth cycle had come full circle.

The Hindu concept of *Siva, Brahma,* and *Vishnu* may be present on *Sgt. Pepper's* cover. *Siva* is the power of creation and destruction as evidenced in the cycle of birth, death, and rebirth; *Brahma* represents the power of the mind and serves as creator of the world; and *Vishnu* represents salvation, and offers protection for man against evil. In his tenth incarnation, *Vishnu* will destroy the earth and end the cycle of birth, death, and rebirth for all time, as witnessed by the Hindu faith.

James Joyce and T. S. Eliot were both influenced by the Fisher King legends and the cycle of birth, death, and rebirth. One of Joyce's concepts in *Finnegans Wake* was presenting a cyclical theory of history. This theory was first presented in 1725 by the Italian philosopher Giambattista Vico. Vico wrote that history passed through four phases:

1. The divine or theocratic, in which man was governed by his belief and acceptance of the su-

pernatural. In this state, the worship of fertility gods explained the changing of the seasons and was represented in the coming of winter. Legends have existed throughout history that used the belief that a god's death directly brought about the hardships of the winter season. When the climate turned warmer and life began anew, the old god was said to have been reborn. Man's acceptance of this cycle developed his faith and, in return, led to the development of religion itself.

2. The aristocratic stage is represented in the Heroic Age of Homer and in the development of the traditional epics, with great kings and mighty warriors who govern mankind wisely. Many of these classical heros would themselves be reborn as gods following their tragic deaths.

3. The democratic and individualistic stage is the complete absence of heroes and with mankind sharing in self-rule. In this stage, mankind stagnates into a wasteland, and awaits the final stage of history.

4. The final stage of chaos is represented by man's fall into confusion. With nothing more to believe in, man will again turn to the supernatural and the cycle will begin anew.

(*The Norton Anthology of English Literature*, 1968)

James Joyce, William Butler Yeats, and T. S. Eliot were convinced that their generation was in this final stage of chaos, awaiting the sudden shock that would start the process all over again. T. S. Eliot's *Wasteland* conforms to this premise. In Eliot's *The Hollow Men*, the human race becomes blind both spiritually and physically and is unable and unworthy to complete the quest for salvation.

Surprisingly, the Beatles' death clues had followed the metaphysical direction of Joyce, Yeats, and Eliot. Their existence as a group bore a resemblance to Vico's statement about history. At first, some individuals referred to the Beatles as supernatural deities. The blind, sick, and crippled reached out to touch the group in search of a miracle. The Beatles became legends overnight.

When the death clues first emerged, adoring fans spread the news of the tragic fate of McCartney to other believers, in much the same way as the news of John Kennedy's assassination had spread. In this way, the Beatles became the epic heroes for a twentieth-century audience.

The Beatles underwent Vico's democratic and individualistic phase after the death of Brian Epstein. The Beatles ruled themselves, though not very successfully, and underwent a glorious evolution into four talented individuals who could no longer fit the demands of a group. The Beatles, now locked in chaos, awaited the final stage, the shock that would start the endless cycle once again.

Vico sincerely believed that a shift through these historic stages would be preceded by a deafening crash of thunder. In Joyce's *Finnegans Wake*, there are instances of long multi-syllabic words used to duplicate Vico's thunder crash. For instance, Joyce includes this description at the very beginning of his masterpiece: "The fall (bababadalgharaghtakamminarronnkonnbronntonnerronntuonnthunntrovarrhounawnskawntoohoohoordenenthurnuk)!"

This thunderlike phrase suggested a shift through one of Vico's four stages of history. Since the Beatles, especially McCartney, considered *Sgt. Pepper's Lonely Heart Club Band* the forerunner of a new age in music, it would be appropriate for them to end the album with their own thundrous crash to signal the birth of a new age.

In *It Was Twenty Years Ago Today*, Derek Taylor described the orchestral crescendo at the conclusion of "A Day in the Life." All four Beatles, along with George Martin, simultaneously struck an E major chord upon three pianos. The engineer pushed the mixer faders down at the precise moment the chords were struck. As the sound slowly faded, the faders were then slowly pushed all the way up. "In all it took forty-five seconds and it was done three or four times piling on a huge sound." This reverberating E major chord concludes the *Sgt. Pepper's Lonely Hearts Club Band* album and, like a burst of thunder, propels the listener into a new age of musical enlightenment.

In David Sheff's *The Playboy Interviews with John Lennon and Yoko Ono*, Sheff asked Lennon one simple question: What was his prescription of life? Lennon answered that we must make our own dreams. That is just what the Beatles did. You have to do it for yourself. No one else can do it for you. Since the beginning of time, the great, enlightened leaders have shown mankind the way, but man does not accept the message. There is nothing new, and no one can provide the answer for you but yourself. "I can't wake you up. You can wake you up. I can't cure you. You can cure you." What keeps us from accepting this message is simply fear of the unknown. This fear sends us chasing around in circles following dreams and illusions. "Everything is unknown—then you are ahead of the game. That's what it is, right?"

CHAPTER 10

Paul
Is
Dead

AND THE ANSWER IS . . .

Obviously, there are many unanswered questions concerning the "Paul is dead" mystery. One of the first riddles involves the rumor's inception in Detroit, Michigan.

When the Beatles landed in America and attended their first press conference, the first question was, naturally, "When are you going to get a haircut?" The second question was, "What about the campaign in Detroit to stamp out the Beatles?" to which Paul responded, "We've got a campaign of our own to stamp out Detroit."

With this in mind, it seems both ironic and appropriate that death rumors would leak from the city that sought the Beatles' end. The mystery caller remains unidentified. Perhaps it was one of the Beatles themselves who broke the tragic news, or their press agent Derek Taylor who simply followed Paul's request to "Let it go." But the rumor snowballed and gained momentum. *Sgt. Pepper's Lonely Heart's Club Band* was resurrected by the record-buying public as the search for the death clues intensified. The White Album and *Abbey Road* continued their already brisk sales and brought in more revenue for the Apple coffers. Was it only a coincidence that Apple was in such dire financial trouble, and that the death-clue hysteria helped generate the enormous amounts of income needed to meet the Beatles' everyday expenses and pay their debts? If this were true, then the clever marketing of the death clues was extremely successful.

Robey Younge (WABC) offered this thought almost thirty years later: "Why would the Beatles have done this? Was it because it was a very fabulous income producing situation for Great Britain? I mean, it brought in a lot of money from all over the world, and if one of the boys was maimed, as they said, in a car crash coming home from the studio early one morning, and had been burned in a fire and was terribly disfigured, wouldn't it behoove them to get someone else who looked similar and was talented also enough to keep the group together, and keep the millions and eventually billions of dollars coming in to EMI and Thorn Industries? Well, maybe they did that. I don't know. They sold a lot of albums because of that and the reason was I happened to be on a very powerful station at that time. I haven't made up my mind yet. I haven't said he was dead, but I said there is reason to believe that something is going on. I think it came from within the inner circle of George Martin, the engineers in the studio, and the Beatles themselves, who resented being totally controlled by the people who obviously controlled them, and they wanted to let it out secretly. So, they did what engineers and writers sometimes do, they mixed it in. And then later, much later, it all began to come out. And then they denied it, why not? They made their money, and the rest, as they say, is history."

Perhaps the whole controversy was only a coincidence. Maybe the public only found clues that coincided with what they wanted to find. The seekers saw what they wanted to see and heard what they wanted to hear. However, there were far too many staged clues for an answer as simple as this. Obviously, there were a number of clues that were created by a number of radio personalities to help perpetuate the myth. These clues, however, tended for the most part to be very farfetched and, with careful listening, easily discredited.

Most likely, investigators had stumbled onto the greatest hoax since the Halloween broadcast of Orson Welles' *The War of the Worlds*. But, come to think of it, in which month were the clues first presented? The answer, of course, is October, the same month that Welles broadcast the supposed invasion of earth by Martians. The hysteria generated by both events is very similar. What's more, the first death clues were presented during the Halloween season—a holiday that is not only famous for trickery, but also associated with the death of the fertility god, the Fisher King.

Paul McCartney held his press conference in November to announce his well-being. Of course, November is the month of Thanksgiving, and a vast majority of the public gave thanks for McCartney's good health, and decided that the "Paul is dead" rumor was exactly that.

As the month of December approached and visions of Christmas season filled the public mind, it now appeared obvious that the symbolic cycle was now complete, since Christmas is associated with the birth of Christ. The timing could have been mere coincidence, but it fit with the concept of the Fisher King legend, and helped fulfill the archetypal religious doctrine of birth, death, and rebirth or, in this case, resurrection. In this way, Lennon could have easily demonstrated that at least, archetypally, the Beatles were every bit as popular as Jesus Christ to their worshiping audience.

If the Beatles did not stage a religious parody, then perhaps the answer to their silence concerning the death clues lay in the investigation of the Charles Manson family. Today, there have been many attempts to hold rock groups accountable for their tremendous influence over adoring fans. Recently, civil lawsuits have been filed against Ozzy Osborne and Judas Priest concerning the effects of their songs upon impressionable young fans. If rock lyrics and hidden messages result in a drastic change in human behavior, specifically attempted suicide, then the offending musicians may very well be charged with numerous civil indictments. If found guilty of such a conspiracy, millions of dollars could be at stake.

Maybe it was jut another coincidence that the "Paul is dead" rumors came to an abrupt halt after the "Helter Skelter" murders. Perhaps the Beatles became concerned that if they admitted to planting clues they could very well be charged in some sort of conspiracy that would indirectly link them to the Manson murders. Perhaps it would be much safer to give up the hoax and deny it ever happened. This way, the Beatles would be safe from any lawsuit implicating the band members.

Maybe the joke had simply gotten out of hand, and they felt it was better to cut their losses rather than risk involvement by stating that cryptic clues and backward messages did exist on their recordings.

One other puzzling thought lingered about the hoax concept. The Beatles, to this day, have stated that the whole search for the death clues was merely a coincidence, and that the clues meant nothing. If a hoax was truly played upon the public, why haven't the surviving Beatles revealed the true details behind the hoax's conception?

As the Christmas holiday season of 1969 passed quietly, and a new year presented itself, filled with promise that the Vietnam War would soon end, and that the world would finally know peace, American television sets glowed on the cold winter night of February 23, 1970. It was a little over six years since the Beatles had made their first appearance on *The Ed Sullivan Show.* One program playing that night was *Rowan and Martin's Laugh In,* and it contained the following lines in a skit involving two angels in heaven:

> ANGEL ONE: Is there any truth to the rumor that Paul McCartney is still alive?
> ANGEL TWO: I doubt it. Where do you think we get those groovy harp arrangements?

CHAPTER II

The
Ultimate
Beatle
Death-Clue
Quiz

 After reading the many clues in this book, it is time for you, dear reader, to try your hand at answering some trivia questions. See if you can earn your doctorate in Beatlemania by answering the following questions:

1. Where can the clue "Paul?" be found?
2. Give three interpretations for the fade-out message at the conclusion of "Strawberry Fields Forever."
3. In which Beatles' video does Ringo play a bass drum that reads "Love 3 Beatles"?
4. What did the word *walrus* supposedly represent to investigators?
5. What did the open hand over Paul's head on the cover of *Sgt. Pepper's Lonely Hearts Club Band* suggest?

6. Which famous attorney conducted a television hearing exploring the infamous death clues?

7. What was the day, month, and year of the tragic accident that supposedly claimed Paul McCartney?

8. Which DJ in Detroit, Michigan, broke the death clues to an unsuspecting world?

9. In which Beatles' song can a listener hear Lennon state that "Paul is dead now, miss him, miss him, miss him!" (Remember the track must be played backward!)?

10. Who is Joe Ephgrave?

11. In which song does Ringo state, "You were in a car crash and you lost your hair"?

12. What is the importance of the message "BE AT LESO?"

13. Who was the mysterious girl Paul was with the night of the accident? Remember, he "took her home [and he] nearly made it."

14. What is the symbolism behind the black walrus?

15. Give three reasons that John Lennon couldn't have been the walrus.

16. What automobile was McCartney driving the night of the accident? On which album jacket does this car appear?

17. What Shakespearean play is heard during the fade-out of "I Am the Walrus"?

18. In which Beatles' song does John Lennon sing of a mysterious victim who "blew his mind out in a car"?

19. George Harrison supposedly moans Paul's name over and over in the fade-out of which Beatles' classic?

20. On "Revolution 9," the engineer's voice repeats "Number nine, number nine" over and over. What does the voice say when the track is reversed?

21. Why is Paul's back turned to the camera on the back side of *Sgt. Pepper's Lonely Hearts Club Band?*

22. Give three clues that suggest that it is Paul in the black walrus suit on the cover of the *Magical Mystery Tour.*

23. What significance do the death clues borrow from Edgar Allan Poe, Lewis Carroll, William Shakespeare, Carl Jung, and James Joyce?

24. What is the symbolism behind the number nine? How does it relate to John Lennon?

25. What is the purpose of the line, "Monsieur, Monsieur, how about another one?"

26. Explain the importance of "LMW 28IF."

27. On which album cover do investigators claim a mysterious phone number is given to help explain the tragic fate of Paul McCartney?

28. Where is the hidden death's head on the back of *Abbey Road?*

29. Which death clue is associated with "connect the dots"?

30. What is the name of the mysterious double who was said to have taken Paul McCartney's place?

31. Which investigator flew to England, and claimed that the only way he would believe that Paul McCartney was still alive would be if Paul's fingerprints matched his 1965 passport?

32. Where do we find the death clue "I was"?

33. Who knows "what it's like to be dead"?

34. What do the liner photos from the White Album seem to suggest?

35. How do the Beatle death clues relate to the Fisher King symbol?

36. In which Beatles' song does John Lennon state that "one and one and one is three"?

37. Give the two death clues associated with *Life* magazine's cover photo and "The Magical McCartney Mystery" article.

38. Explain the hidden meaning behind the *Abbey Road* cover.

39. What interpretation is made of the White Album cover-art design?

40. How many Beatles' songs refer to mysterious car accidents?

41. Describe the hidden death clues behind *The Beatles Yesterday . . . and Today* album.

42. In which song does Lennon state that "the walrus was Paul"?

43. Which album cover contains a series of dots that, when connected, reveals the hidden message "3 Beatles"?

44. Compare the Beatle death clues to James Joyce's *Finnegans Wake*.

45. What death clue is associated with *Rubber Soul*?

46. What death clue is associated with *Revolver?*

47. What role did Charles Manson play in hidden Beatles' messages?

48. What message is spelled out in yellow hyacinths on *Sgt. Pepper's* cover?

49. Where is the line, "So alright Paul we had better go and see a surgeon" found?

50. Where can Paul be seen wearing a black carnation?

51. In this liner photo, Paul is seen lying back in a bathtub. This was supposed to represent McCartney as a headless corpse. Where is this photo found?

52. What is the significance of the OPD arm patch found on the inside of *Sgt. Pepper's Lonely Hearts Club Band?*

53. What color is the back of *Sgt. Pepper's* jacket? What does this supposedly represent?

54. According to *Life* magazine, a sonogram was made comparing Paul's voice in separate vocal arrangements. What were the results of this study?

55. Where can a listener discern, "Let me out! Let me out!"?

56. What is the basic idea behind the conspiracy and coverup involving the "Paul is dead" rumor?

57. Which song, played backward, of course, seems to say "Turn me on, dead man"?

58. On which Beatles' song fade-out can the following messages be heard: "Bury my body," "O, untimely death," and "What, Is he dead?

59. In which Beatles' song is Paul's double introduced for the first time?

60. What is the hidden meaning of the eggman's "goo goo g'joob"?

61. Where can one find Paul's bloody shoes?

62. Where can one find a bloodstained driving glove?

63. Where, on *Sgt. Pepper's* cover, is the flaming car?

64. What is the meaning behind the *Let It Be* cover?

65. In which song does John ask us to "look through the bent back tulips"?

66. What is the purpose of John "fixing a hole in the ocean"?

67. What does the 1966 Beatles release *Oldies* suggest?

68. What clue suggests that the death hoax was intended for American audiences?

69. How do the songs "How Do You Sleep" and "Back off Boogaloo" relate to the "Paul is dead" conspiracy?

70. Give the coincidence behind Paul's *Red Rose Speedway, Flowers in the Dirt,* and *Paul Is Live.*

71. What death clues are associated with the "Butcher Cover"?

72. What does the empty bowl of cherries from the *McCartney* solo album suggest?

73. Which Beatles song mentions a day when papers didn't come?

74. What similarities can be found connecting the "Paul is dead" rumor to the OJ Simpson case?

75. Where can a listener find the hidden message "Paul is bloody . . . Paul is very bloody"?

76. What is the irony behind Paul's barefoot walk across Abbey Road?

77. Name the city where the "Paul is dead" rumors began. Why is this significant?

78. What could Paul McCartney's solo album *Flowers in the Dirt* be a reference to?

79. What supposedly became of Jane Asher, Paul's one-time fiancée?

80. Cite one death clue on McCartney's *Off the Ground* album.

81. What is strange about the background of Paul's photograph on *Let It Be?*

82. What does each Beatle supposedly represent on *Abbey Road?*

83. What instrument does McCartney hold on *Sgt. Pepper's* cover? Why is this unusual?

84. What did some sleuths make of Wings, the name of McCartney's band?

85. Give two explanations for Paul's position (facing the camera directly) on *Sgt. Pepper's.*

86. The end chord on *Sgt. Pepper's* is symbolic of what?

87. Where can McCartney be found in the fetal position?

88. What clues can be associated with Apple Corps?

89. How are the drum from *Sgt. Pepper's* and the onion ("Glass Onion") similar? How does this relate to Lewis Carroll?

90. What is the imperfection in "Beatles" on the back of *Abbey Road?*

91. Where does McCartney appear with scars above his upper lip?

92. Who was Billy Shears? What did many fans consider him?

93. What is the M&D Company?

94. Where does Paul appear in a "coffin"?

95. Why did Paul grow a mustache for *Sgt. Pepper's?*

96. "Come Together" possibly refers to what scene?

97. What is significant about "Beatles," as opposed to "The Beatles"?

98. How do death-clue researchers interpret the blurred image on the back of *Abbey Road?*

99. What is significant about the guitar strings on *Sgt. Pepper's?*

100. How did the epaulets the Beatles wear on *Sgt. Pepper's* contribute to the death-clue hysteria?

101. Where does the image of the flaming car appear?

102. What do the nautical voices in "Yellow Submarine" seem to say?

103. In "Only a Northern Song," of what does George Harrison warn the listener?

104. Were any hidden messages placed in Morse Code? Where is it said to be found?

105. Are there any death clues from the "Free as a Bird" video? Where are they found?

106. What is the meaning behind "Turned out nice again"?

107. In which song from *Anthology 3* can one hear a voice that says "Help"?

108. What is the significance of the *Anthology 3* album cover as it relates to the death-clue hysteria?

109. Are there death clues in the "Yellow Submarine" movie? Where are they?

110. How many hidden Beatle references can you find in the "Free as a Bird" video?

EPILOGUE

From *Paul Is Live* Through the *Anthologies*

It is difficult to believe that it has now been over thirty years since "Sergeant Pepper taught the band to play." In 1992, Paul McCartney celebrated his fiftieth birthday. The colors silver and gold do well to describe the ageless melodic sounds of the still-Fab Four. Hopefully, my work will help encourage others to explore and enjoy the collected works of John Lennon, Paul McCartney, George Harrison, and Ringo Starr.

It is intriguing that the Beatles still refuse to comment on the death hoax. In my opinion, it is indisputable that McCartney continues to perpetuate the death-clue rumors through his song and album covers. (Some fans even suggested that the name of Paul McCartney's band, Wings, conjured up images of dying, angels, and heaven.) As proof of his willingness to incorporate hidden messages within his albums, McCartney included a message in Braille on his *Red Rose Speedway* album. The message, intended for Stevie Wonder, read, "We love you, Stevie, baby."

McCartney's album *Flowers in the Dirt* seemed to hint at a longing remembrance of a time of marching bands and girls with kaleidoscope eyes. Perhaps *Flowers in the Dirt* jokingly refers to the yellow-hyacinth guitar placed upon a freshly dug grave. ("Paul?") McCartney's album *Off the Ground* featured six pairs of bare feet, perhaps reminiscent of the famous walk across Abbey Road. In late 1993, McCartney released a new work entitled, appropriately enough, *Paul Is Live.* On the cover, Paul duplicates his infamous walk across Abbey Road. This time, instead of being part of a funeral procession, Paul is leading an English sheepdog across the notorious crosswalk. Perhaps there *is* a double in this picture. Not McCartney, however, but Martha, the sheepdog remembered fondly in "Martha My Dear." According to *Club Sandwich*, the McCartney official fan newsletter, this particular sheepdog's name is Arrow and belongs to Paul's son, James.

McCartney paid painstakingly close attention to every detail in creating this parody. The original *Abbey Road* photographer, Iain Macmillan, took the shot on July 22, 1993. Paul wore a suit made by Edward Sexton, the same tailor who made the suit he wore on the *Abbey Road* cover. The computer-generated scene (it was impossible to make the zebra crossing stripes match the original photo) is complete with another Volkswagen Beetle parked alongside the curb, with a license plate that reads "51 IS," which refers to the fact that Paul McCartney is still alive and rocking to this very day. But, in a world of computer generated graphics and high technology, anything is possible.

A great and, many Beatle fans feel, long-overdue honor was granted to Paul McCartney on Tuesday March 11, 1997, when Queen Elizabeth knighted him. The ceremony took place at Buckingham Palace, and obviously brought back memories of the day the Beatles received their M.B.E. (Member of the British

Empire) medals. As the soon-to-be-knighted Sir Paul arrived giving his fans a thumbs-up sign, the crowd broke into spontaneous arrangements of "Hey Jude," "A Hard Day's Night," and a parody of McCartney's timeless classic "Yesterday." The crowd changed the lyrics to "Yes Sir Day." Somehow, John Lennon must have been smiling down. As far as George Harrison and Ringo Starr's reactions to the investiture service, Paul simply stated that he had received a number of phone calls from his fellow Beatles who simply referred to him as "Your Holiness." In an interview with the London *Sun*, a deeply moved McCartney stated, "This is the best day of my life. Coming from a terraced house in Liverpool to this house (Buckingham Palace) is quite a journey and I am immensely proud. . . . Today is fantastic, there is a blue sky and it's springtime. My mum and dad would have been extremely proud today—and perhaps they were."

Perhaps this honor was prompted by an event that Beatles' fans worldwide had been hoping for ever since 1970—the Beatles getting back together. In 1995, Capitol Records announced plans for the release of three double-CD sets. The *Anthologies* were to be produced and compiled by original producer George Martin and the three surviving Beatles. Over 400 hours of outtakes were searched to provide an adequate history of the Fab Four. In November, ABC arranged for a special Beatles' *Anthology* that would last for three nights and be aired in prime time. It was to be the Beatles' story told by the Beatles themselves. I, by chance, was lucky enough to watch the first *Anthology* broadcast at the Fab Four Fest in Atlanta, Georgia. My good friend Michelle Harper had arranged for the show and, by complete happenstance, ABC had chosen that Sunday night to air the first night's special. It was a very special time to share Beatles' memories with a crowd of a hundred other Beatle fans who cheered and clapped their hands throughout the entire show. The first night's program ended with the airing of the first new Beatles' song in over twenty-five years. Through the miracle of modern technology, John Lennon's 1980 demo "Free as a Bird" was re-recorded with the other three Beatles adding their parts. According to Paul McCartney, the game plan was to pretend that John had simply gone on holiday and had left them to finish the musical composition. The finished product was haunting. John's voice took the lead vocal track with Paul coming in on the chorus. The harmonies were stunning, and the Beatles sounded as if they had never left us. The sales of the first *Anthology* was sheer Beatlemania all over again. According to Capitol records, *Anthology 1* sold 450,000 copies on its first day of release. Many music stores opened at midnight, as anxious customers waited in long lines to purchase the first Beatles' offering. The first weeks' sales were given as 855,000 copies. This was a phenomenal number, given the fact that a great majority of the cuts were outtakes. *Variety* stated that *Anthology 2* sold 441,000 copies in the first week of release, while *Anthology 3* sold 238,000 units during its first week sales. It seems that every band since the Beatles has a burning desire to be "bigger than the Beatles." It was only appropriate that this feat would be accomplished by the three surviving members with the release of the long-awaited *Anthology* collections.

With the first installment of *Anthology*, many fans were stunned to find yet another chapter to the hidden Beatles' symbolism. According to media sources, the Beatles placed more than eighty visual references to song lyrics and their personal lives into the "Free as a Bird" video. It seems that, once again, the Beatles encouraged us to roll up for yet another journey into a never-ending mystery tour. Step right this way!

The "Free as a Bird" video begins with what appears to be

an interior shot that could well suggest John's Dakota apartment. On the mantlepiece, we can see photos of each of the Beatles as children—each member pictured in the perpetual, childlike innocence that belies the advent of fame and fortune. Placed upon the mantle are the figures of two insects, a fly and a butterfly. Perhaps this was a tongue-in-cheek reference to another member of the insect family, the beetles. As we listen carefully, an unseen presence, with the sound of a bird in flight, invokes memories of blackbirds and the faraway, dreamlike idyll of Norwegian wood. Just as the vision captures our imagination, we burst from the room, synchronized in perfect time with the soaring melodic strains of George Harrison's slide guitar. Now, we are gliding in surrealistic flight above the working-class dwellings of Liverpool. This whole experience brings to mind the musical composition "Flying" found on the *Magical Mystery Tour* album, and credited to all four musicians. In the span of a few seconds, we have been introduced to images suggesting "Norwegian Wood" (remember the subtitle "the bird has flown," which is exactly what we do as the camera pans over the city rooftops), "Blackbird," and "Across the Universe" (in both cases the recorded sound effects contained within the Abbey Road studio vaults).

As the camera glides over what appears to be the city of Liverpool, we see images of what appears to be a boat on a river ("picture yourself on a boat on a river," from "Lucy in The Sky With Diamonds") and, finally, we land in Penny Lane. This, of course, is a direct reference to Paul McCartney's tribute to his old neighborhood. In the first scene, we see the Beatles joining dock workers in the pouring rain ("when the rain comes they run and hide their heads," from "Rain;" "the pouring rain," from "Penny Lane;" and "get your tan from standing in the English rain," from "I Am the Walrus"). There is a crowd pushing fran-

tically to enter the Cavern. When the Beatles are seen performing on the small stage, they appear to be doing one of their early
trademark songs, "Some Other Guy."

Next, the camera focuses on the gates of Strawberry Fields.
A solitary figure, John Lennon, is seen strolling leisurely
through the opened gates. In the next scene, children run about,
some hand in hand ("I Want to Hold Your Hand"), and one boy
later whispers in a girl's ear ("Let me whisper in your ear," from
"Listen! Do You Want to Know a Secret?"). The children are in
what appears to be a marketplace, perhaps suggesting the off-
spring of Desmond and Molly Jones ("Ob La Di Ob La Da").
Also, there is what appears to be Desmond's covered barrow in
this marketplace. A station wagon is sitting alongside the curb
with a painted reference to an egg company. The man selling
the eggs is obviously the eggman, suggesting "I Am the Walrus." Two men resembling former British Prime Ministers Wilson and Heath walk by the crowd ("Tax Man"). A pretty nurse
is selling "poppies from a tray" and, as she stares at the camera,
with a glassy look, she does appear to be "in a play" ("Penny
Lane").

We are also introduced to the barber who has a picture of
"every head he's had the pleasure to know" ("Penny Lane"). A
sign on a wall appears mentioning "Help" as two young girls
are seen leaving a business, one dressed in black ("Baby's in
Black") or perhaps a plasticlike raincoat ("Polythene Pam"). A
couple can be seen making out in a parked car ("Why Don't We
Do It in the Road?") as the Beatles stand by laughing. One of
the buildings has the completed *Anthology* cover in its entirety
pasted upon the rough, brick finish. In the bakery window, we
see a cake that displays "Happy Birthday" ("Birthday") and the
numerals six and four ("When I'm Sixty-Four").

George Harrison then appears, entering the Apple business

offices (taken from the *Let It Be* film), only this time Dr. Robert's name is placed on a sign outside the door. One of the most interesting scenes occurs next. A crowd of people stand and stare at the aftermath of a car accident. John Lennon can be seen gazing from the crowd. Of course, this scene was taken from "A Day in the Life." One strange likeness appears in the wind screen of the police van before the accident scene is visited. With the tape in slow motion, an image that somewhat resembles Paul McCartney, complete with mustache, can be discerned from the mixture of light and shadow. This may well be a stretch, but it would certainly be a clever mention of the death-clue hysteria. When the accident is seen, the car resembles a Lotus. In this case, it would follow the Tara Browne scenario. The crashed car's license plate seems to state "VFE7." Some fans take this to suggest that the Beatles had seven wives between them—VFE (wife) 7. At the accident scene, we see the "pretty little police men in a row" ("I Am the Walrus"), a "clean fire engine" complete with a fireman that "rushes in" ("Penny Lane"), and a girl who is crying as she is being attended to ("Cry Baby Cry").

The next camera angle brings into focus a huge amusement park slide ("Helter Skelter"), and a flying kite ("Being for the Benefit of Mr. Kite"). A small group of children wearing pig masks can be seen running in an alley way ("Piggies"). The Beatles appear behind the children and walk through a "wall of illusion" ("Within You Without You"). A ladder is placed upon a wall and a foot can be seen as it quickly enters through a window ("She Came in Through the Bathroom Window"). Large sunflowers can be seen "growing incredibly high" from the terraced walls. The camera rushes to the outside window of a man who obviously is a "Paperback Writer." If you look closely, there is "a lizard on the windowpane" ("Happiness is a Warm Gun").

As the camera scans the room, a clock can be seen sitting in the bookcase. Its time is 10:10 ("One after 909"). There is a picture of Sir Walter Raleigh placed on the inside of the window ("and curse Sir Walter Raleigh he was such a stupid get," from "I'm So Tired"). A copy of *The Daily Mail* can be seen ("Paperback Writer") lying on the table. Its headline is "4000 HOLES IN BLACKBURN LANCASHIRE" ("A Day in the Life"). Also placed on the table are a small bowl of green apples (Apple Corps, Ltd.) and a box of Savoy Truffles ("Savoy Truffle"). A John Lennon figure reclines in chair ("I'm So Tired," "I'm Only Sleeping") next to a television set that appears to be playing the Beatles' performance on the Ed Sullivan Show. A picture of Queen Elizabeth can be seen resting on the floor ("Her Majesty," or a reference to the MBE medals), and in the window a small picture of Chairman Mao ("Revolution").

The camera then exits the room, and a hole on a neighboring roof is seen being repaired ("Fixing a Hole"). A Blue Meanie is then seen raising its head up through the hole (*Yellow Submarine*). A man walks down the street leading a white bulldog ("Hey Bull Dog"), as a "newspaper taxi" ("Lucy in the Sky with Diamonds") picks up a young lady as its fare ("She's Leaving Home"). Two workmen carry a large poster of Chairman Mao ("Revolution") and John and Yoko waltz by (this dance scene is from the movie *Let It Be*, and takes place to "I Me Mine." It could also represent "The Ballad of John and Yoko"). A Blue Meanie sticks his head up through a hole in the road (*Yellow Submarine* and "Mean Mr. Mustard"; remember, "Mr. Mustard lives in a hole in the road"), and the Magical Mystery Tour bus passes by down the street.

As the next scene approaches, a figure of Napoleon can be quickly seen. (Remember, in the "All You Need Is Love" video, "The Marseillaise," the French national anthem, written during the turbulent French Revolution, serves as the introduction.) This scene appears to take place in the lobby of a grand hotel. A big-game hunter appears from safari, complete with an elephant and "his mother" ("Bungalow Bill"). An Indian musician can be observed playing the sitar (the influence of Ravi Shankar, and a reference to the Beatles' interest in Far Eastern religions). Brian Epstein (the Beatles' manager) can be seen in one of the small groups, as can the Beatles dressed in their *Sgt. Pepper's* finery. A multitude of figures from the *Sgt. Pepper's* cover can be seen. Those figures include H. G. Wells and Lawrence of Arabia. The *Sgt. Pepper's* bass drum is in the center, and a cardboard cutout of James Dean can be seen, but with Stu Sutcliffe's head. John loved Sutcliffe's look. It reminded him of James Dean.

The camera now ascends through a skylight and the sun can be clearly seen ("Here Comes the Sun"). A cemetery can now be examined complete, with a statue of a Madonna figure ("Lady Madonna") that turns its head, and Eleanor Rigby's tombstone. Father McKenzie can be seen as he "walks away from the grave" ("Eleanor Rigby"). A sheepdog then runs playfully by the headstones ("Martha My Dear"). To the left of the screen, Paul appears in a scene from "The Fool on the Hill" video sequence from the *Magical Mystery Tour* film. A long and winding road appears in the background ("Long and Winding Road"), and a young lady with a suitcase walks alongside the road ("She's Leaving Home"). The famous Abbey Road crosswalk (*Abbey Road*) now appears, as a meter maid ("Lovely Rita") tickets the parked Volkswagen (*Abbey Road*).

The last scene displays the Beatles as they appeared in *A Hard Day's Night*, rushing into a theater. Next to the stage door is a clown ("gather 'round all you clowns" from "You've Got to Hide Your Love Away") and, on the stage, is a performer playing a ukelele. At the conclusion of his performance, as the curtain falls ("The End"), a voice appears to be saying, "My name's John Lennon." This is a backward track that when reversed exclaims, "Turned out nice again." This was a tribute to George Formby. Formby was a vaudevillian performer who specialized in the ukelele. It seems that the phrase "Turned out nice again, mama" was one of his trademark lines during live performances. George Harrison is said to be a Formby's fan and collector.

The Beatles' use of a backward track, and the hidden Beatle references in "Free as a Bird" (FAAB) had some fans peering over the *Anthology* artwork to find other hidden allusions. The third *Anthology* cover provided some interesting coincidences. Of course, the *Abbey Road* cover is prominently featured, as well as the word *Remains.* The sinister mentioning of the word *remains,* to some of the more overenthusiastic fans, conjures up the thought of a corpse. The Remains, however, was a rock group led by Barry Tashian, who opened for the Beatles on their last tour. Obviously, there is nothing diabolical here. The most bizarre coincidence concerns the center drawing. The Beatles appear pictured from the *Let It Be* album. There is one difference, however. Three of the Beatles (John, Ringo, and George) are pictured as they appeared on the original *Let It Be* album from 1970. Paul McCartney's photo is, again, different from the others. The McCartney photo was taken from the *Rubber Soul* jacket, and represents Paul McCartney from 1966—the same year as the alleged tragic car crash. Also, during the "Glass Onion" outtake, when John sings about the walrus being Paul, a voice utters a muffled "help." This may represent the Beatles' attempt at knowing humor, to provide yet one more "clue for you all."

Shortly before the release of the *Beatles Anthologies* in October 1995, Paul McCartney chose yet another format to display his wit concerning both backward maskings and the untimely rumors of his tragic demise. During fall 1995, two episodes of *The Simpsons* hint at the rumor. (When Lisa Simpson first meets Paul McCartney, she tells him that she has heard about him in her history class.) All three former Beatles have appeared at one time or another as guests in the popular television series. The first episode, a Halloween special, features a tombstone etched with Paul McCartney's name. In the second episode, an animated Paul and Linda McCartney make a statement concerning their belief in vegetarianism. During the program, Paul states that playing "Maybe I'm Amazed" backwards will yield a "ripping recipe for lentil soup." Sure enough, at the song's conclusion, the fade-out features Paul singing "Maybe I'm Amazed" and, when reversed, the song spells out the ingredients, cup by cup, with a dash of "Sgt. Pepper" to complete the popular vegetarian dish. And, at the conclusion of the backward mask, almost expectedly, he states, "Oh, and by the way—I'm alive."

APPENDIX

The Clues, Album by Album

Rubber Soul: This album contained a sinister reference to "tires" (rubber) and "death" (soul); many fans felt that this reference suggested Paul's death in an automobile accident.

The Beatles Yesterday . . . and Today: This American release hinted that a transition had taken place within the group, and became the first of many strange coincidental album covers suggesting that Paul was dead. *The Beatles Yesterday . . . and Today* contains the following clues:

1. Paul is sitting in an open trunk that resembles a coffin, especially when the cover is turned to the side.
2. Several of the song titles suggested that McCartney was tragically killed in a car accident, e.g., "Drive My Car," "Nowhere Man," "Dr. Robert," "Act Naturally," and so on.
3. The album jacket may well hint at the first cover-up.

Revolver: The title suggested a change, as in a revolving door: One person leaves as another enters. The album cover also suggested that Paul's photo was forced in with the others, since his is in profile.

1. The lyrics to "She Said She Said" contains the mysterious line "I know what it's like to be dead."
2. In the song lyrics to "Got To Get You into My Life" Paul sings, "I was alone, I took a ride, / I didn't know what I would find there." There may well be a play on words when the singer suggests that he must get

someone into his life. Could this mean that an imposter was brought in to take the place of the popular Beatle?

3. The song titles "I Wanna Tell You" and "Tomorrow Never Knows" hint at the supposed tragedy and an effort to reveal it to the public.

Sgt. Pepper's Lonely Hearts Club Band: This album was brimming with cryptic clues.

1. The Beatles stand above a grave on the cover.
2. The hyacinths display a left-handed guitar (Paul's instrument). The arrangement also spells out "Paul?"
3. The bass drum was designed by a Joe Ephgrave (an anagram for epitaph and grave.) When a mirror is placed in the center of LONELY HEARTS a hidden message is revealed: I ONE IX HE ◊ DIE. Interpreted, the message suggested that Eleven Nine (November the ninth) HE (McCartney since the diamond points directly up at him) DIE. There is some evidence that McCartney was actually involved in an automobile crash on this date.
4. On the album cover, there is an open hand above Paul's head. This was interpreted as a symbol of death.
5. The front cover displayed a doll wearing a "Welcome the Rolling Stones" sweatshirt. A model car, which resembled an Aston Martin, the same type of car Paul was driving on the night of his tragic accident, rests on the doll's leg.
6. Paul is playing a black instrument, while the other members are playing golden ones.
7. When the album cover is opened, Paul's arm band displayed the letters OPD—London police jargon for "Officially Pronounced Dead."
8. The back of the album cover is blood red, a color related to the tragic accident.
9. Paul's back is turned toward the camera, striking a different pose. (Many people believed that this was an imposter and, according to some credible sources, they were right!)
10. The song title "Within You Without You" covers Paul's figure with the lyrics suggesting that "We never glimpse the truth until we pass away."
11. George is pointing at a line from the lyric "She's Leaving Home," which reads "Wednesday morning at five o'clock." This was taken to suggest the actual date and time of the accident. Strangely, November 9, 1966, was a Wednesday morning and, according to Beatle sources, Paul was involved in an accident on that day at that precise time.
12. The title song introduced a mysterious Billy Shears, who many fans thought was Paul's double. Some believed that he was a winner of a Paul McCartney look-alike contest, while others thought Billy Shears

was a pseudonym for William Campbell, an actor who, through plastic surgery, was able to take Paul's place in the group.

13. The composition "A Day in the Life" mentioned a person who "blew his mind out in a car / he didn't noticed that the lights had changed / A crowd of people stood and stared / They'd seen his face before." Was this a reference to Paul's accident? In this case, McCartney may have been decapitated, and the viewing public failed to draw the connection to the famous group.

Magical Mystery Tour: What was the mystery that was dying to take us away?

1. The title of the album, when held upside down and observed through a mirror, revealed a telephone number that supposedly enabled the viewer to find the truth about McCartney's death.

2. The Beatles are dressed in animal costumes, one of those being a black walrus, which, in Scandinavian countries, is said to be a symbol of death.

3. The rumor that the word walrus was from the Greek for "corpse" circulated wildly. Thus the song "I Am the Walrus" was translated as "I Am the Corpse."

4. In the lyrics to "I Am the Walrus":
   a. Lennon sang "I am he as you are he as you are me and we are all together." Did this suggest that the Beatles conspired to hide McCartney's death and take his place in the recording studio?
   b. Shakespearean actors recite lines from *King Lear* during the song's fade-out. The lines include: "What, is he dead?" "Bury my body!" "O, untimely death!"

5. During the fade-out and fade-in to "Strawberry Fields Forever" many fans heard an eerie voice exclaim "I buried Paul!"

6. In the song booklet, there are scenes with Paul posed with hands over his head.

7. Paul sits behind a desk with a sign stating, "I Was." He is in military dress, and the British flags are crossed in the proper position for military funerals.

8. During the song "Your Mother Should Know," the Beatles descended a spiral staircase. John, George, and Ringo wore red carnations, while Paul wore a black carnation, which many believed was another symbol of death.

9. The line "Goo goo g'joob" from "I Am the Walrus" is reportedly taken from James Joyce's *Finnegans Wake,* and was said to be the last words of the eggman (Humpty Dumpty) before his famous accident.

10. The line "Stupid bloody Tuesday" from "I Am the Walrus" hinted at

the night Paul angrily left Abbey Road studios right before the tragic accident early the next morning (Wednesday, November 9, 1966).

The Beatles (the White Album): This double album contained the following clues.

1. The close-up photos of the Beatles differed again, with Paul displaying mysterious scars around his upper lip that had not been noticed before. Were these the marks left behind by plastic surgery?
2. On the fold-out lyric sheet, there is a picture of Paul lying back in a bathtub. Many felt that this suggested Paul's death, and that the waters that covered his neck again meant that he had been decapitated.
3. Again, on the fold-out sheet, there is a photo of McCartney with eerie skeletal hands reaching out to ensnare him.
4. The soft muttering right before "Blackbird," when played backward, seems to say "Paul is dead now, miss him, miss him, miss him!"
5. When "Revolution 9" is reversed, the listener hears the sounds of a flaming automobile crash with the victim screaming "Let me out!" The phrase "Number nine" is reversed to reveal the passage "Turn me on deadman."
6. In the song "Glass Onion," John stated "Here's another clue for you all . . . the walrus was Paul!"
7. During "Don't Pass Me By," Ringo sang, "I'm sorry that I doubted you / I was so unfair / You were in a car crash / And you lost your hair." This was taken as another reference to Paul's accidental death.
8. "Blackbirds" have always been symbolic of approaching death and disaster.
9. The color white is the color of mourning in many Far Eastern societies.
10. On "While My Guitar Gently Weeps," it sounds like George moans "Paul, Paul" over and over again during the fade-out. Also, the first vocal sound, when reversed, sounds like "Help."

Abbey Road: The following clues are given.

1. The Beatles represented a funeral procession, with Lennon being religion or God Himself; Ringo, the church (minister) or perhaps the undertaker; Paul, the barefooted corpse, since many societies bury their dead without shoes; and George represented the gravedigger in his work clothes.
2. Paul is out of step with the others.
3. A Volkswagen Beetle's license plate read "28 IF," a reference to McCartney's age if he had lived.
4. The imposter Paul is holding a cigarette in his right hand, whereas the actual McCartney was left-handed.

R. GARY PATTERSON

5. The back of the album contained the word Beatles written on a wall. There is a small crack running through the S, which suggested that there was a flaw within the band.
6. A series of dots before the Beatles sign, if connected, form the number three, which suggested that there were three Beatles (but there are four on the cover!).
7. There is a skull displayed in light and shadow, and tilted at an angle following the Beatles sign.
8. The girl in the blue dress was said to be Jane Asher, Paul's long-time fiancée, who was secretly paid not to reveal the terrible secret.
9. In the song "Come Together," Lennon sang, "One and one and one is three" which again referred to the Beatles as a three-man group.
10. The song "Come Together" may have referred to a wake held over a coffin, when the mourners "come together over me!"

Let It Be: The last released Beatle album (1970).

1. This album is designed in the appropriate color for a funeral, black.
2. Notice that John, George, and Ringo are shown in profile, each looking to the left, whereas McCartney is photographed looking straight into the camera with a blood-red background.
3. "You Know My Name (Look up the Number)," the flip side of the "Let It Be" single, contained the sounds of a cuckoo clock. When the cuckoo chirps five times, a phone number is then mentioned. Some investigaters claim that when the number was dialed a voice answered and replied "Beware of Abbey Road."

Earlier, long before the hysteria, the Beatles recorded "I'm Looking Through You." Though the song was recorded before November 9, 1966, there is still a haunting lyric that stated, "You don't look different, but you have changed / I'm looking through you, you're not the same." According to Beatles' historians this lyric was written for Jane Asher, but still. . . ?

197

BIBLIOGRAPHY

Abrams, M. H., ed. *The Norton Anthology of English Literature.* New York: W.W. Norton & Company, Inc., 1968.

Brown, Peter and Stephen Gaines. *The Love You Make: An Insider's Story of the Beatles.* New York: Penguin Books, New American Library, 1983.

Bugliosi, Vincent and Curt Gentry. *Helter Skelter.* New York: Bantam Books, 1975.

Campbell, John and Henry Mordon Robinson. *A Skeleton Key to Finnegans Wake.* New York: Harcourt Brace & Company, 1944.

Carroll, Lewis. *The Complete Works of Lewis Carroll.* New York: Random House Inc., The Modern Library, 1916.

Cirlot, J. E. *Dictionary of Symbols,* trans. Jack Sage. New York: Philosophical Library, 1971.

Coleman, Ray. *Lennon.* New York: McGraw-Hill, 1985.

Dowlding, William. *Beatlesongs.* New York: Simon & Schuster, Fireside, 1983.

Fawcett, Anthony. *John Lennon: One Day at a Time.* New York: Grove Press, 1976.

Fulpens, H. V. *The Beatles: An Illustrated Diary.* New York: Perigee Books, 1982.

Gaines, Steven. *Heroes and Villains: The True Story of the Beach Boys.* New York: Penguin Books, New American Library, 1986.

Gaskell, G. A. *Dictionary of All Scriptures and Myths.* New York: Julian Press, Avenel Books, 1981.

Goldman, Albert. *The Lives of John Lennon.* New York: William Morrow & Company, Inc., 1988.

Harrison, George, with Derek Taylor. *I Me Mine*. New York: Simon and Schuster, 1980.

Hockinson, Michael J. *The Ultimate Beatles Quiz Book*. New York: St. Martin's Press, 1992.

Jobes, Gertrude. *Dictionary of Mythology, Folklore, and Symbols: Part One*. New York: The Scarecrow Press, Inc. 1962.

Joyce, James. *Finnegans Wake*. New York: Viking Press, 1939.

Lewisohn, Mark. *The Beatles: Recording Sessions*. New York: Harmony Books, 1988.

McCabe, Peter and Robert D. Schonfeld. *Apple to the Core*. New York: Pocket Books, 1972.

McCartney, Michael. *The Macs: Mike McCartney's Family Album*. New York: Delilah Books, 1972.

Marsh, David and Kevin Stein. *The Book of Rock Lists*. New York: Dell/Rolling Stone Press, 1981.

Neary, John. "The Magical McCartney Mystery," *Life*, November 7, 1969.

Norman, Philip. *Shout! The Beatles in Their Generation*. New York: Warner Books, 1982.

Poundstone, William. *Big Secrets*. New York: Quill, 1983.

Riley, Tim. *Tell Me Why: A Beatles Commentary*. New York: Alfred A. Knopf, 1988.

Salewicz, Tim. *McCartney*. New York: St. Martin's Press, 1986.

Schaffner, Nicholas. *The Beatles Forever*. New York: McGraw-Hill, 1978.

Schultheiss, Tom. *A Day in the Life: The Beatles Day-by-Day, 1960–1970*. Ann Arbor, Michigan: Pierian Press, 1980.

Sheff, David. *Playboy Interviews with John Lennon & Yoko Ono*. New York: Berkley Books, 1981.

Shotton, Pete with Nicholas Schaffner. *The Beatles, Lennon and Me*. New York: Stein and Day, 1984.

Stannard, Neville. *The Long and Winding Road: A History of the Beatles on Record*. New York: Avon Books, 1984.

Suczek, Barbara. "The Curious Case of the Death of Paul McCartney." *Urban Life and Culture*. Vol. 1. Beverly Hills: Sage Publications, 1972.

Taylor, Derek. *It Was Twenty Years Ago Today*. New York: Simon & Schuster, Fireside, 1987.

Other articles are taken from assorted CD liner notes, newspaper, and magazine sources, and are documented throughout the work. All album photos are copyright by Apple Corps, Ltd., and EMI/Capitol. All lyrics written by the Beatles and are credited where used: Lennon and McCartney; Harrison; and Starr.

"A Day in the Life," words and music by John Lennon and Paul McCartney. Album: *Sgt. Pepper's Lonely Hearts Club Band* © Northern Songs, 1967.

"Baby You're a Rich Man," words and music by John Lennon and Paul McCartney. Album: *Magical Mystery Tour* © Northern Songs, 1967.

"Back Off Boogaloo," words and music by Richard Starkey. Album: *Blast from Your Past* © Startling Music, Ltd., 1972.

"Blackbird," words and music by John Lennon and Paul McCartney. Album: *The Beatles* (the White Album) © Northern Songs, 1968.

"Come Together," words and music by John Lennon and Paul McCartney. Album: *Abbey Road* © Northern Songs, 1969.

"Don't Pass Me By," words and music by Ringo Starr. Album: *The Beatles* (the White Album) © Sterling Music Limited, 1968.

"Drive My Car," words and music by John Lennon and Paul McCartney. Album: *Yesterday and Today* © Northern Songs, 1965.

"Glass Onion," words and music by John Lennon and Paul McCartney. Album: *The Beatles* (the White Album) © Northern Songs, 1968.

"Good Morning Good Morning," words and music by John Lennon and Paul McCartney. Album: *Sgt. Pepper's Lonely Hearts Club Band* © Northern Songs, 1967.

"Got to Get You into My Life," words and music by John Lennon and Paul McCartney. Album: *Revolver* © Northern Songs, 1966.

"Happiness Is a Warm Gun," words and music by John Lennon and Paul McCartney. Album: *The Beatles* (the White Album) © Northern Songs, 1968.

"Hello Goodbye," words and music by John Lennon and Paul McCartney. Album: *Magical Mystery Tour* © Northern Songs, 1967.

"Helter Skelter," words and music by John Lennon and Paul McCartney. Album: *The Beatles* (the White Album) © Northern Songs, 1968.

"Honey Pie," words and music by John Lennon and Paul McCartney. Album: *The Beatles* (the White Album) © Northern Songs, 1968.

"How Do You Sleep," words and music by John Lennon & Yoko Ono. Album: *Imagine* © Maclen Ono Music, 1971.

"I Am the Walrus," words and music by John Lennon and Paul McCartney. Album: *Magical Mystery Tour* © Northern Songs, 1967.

"I'm Looking Through You," words and music by John Lennon and Paul McCartney. Album: *Rubber Soul* © Northen Songs, 1965.

"I'm So Tired," words and music by John Lennon and Paul McCartney. Album: *The Beatles* (the White Album) © Northern Songs, 1968.

"Lovely Rita," words and music by John Lennon and Paul McCartney. Album: *Sgt. Pepper's Lonely Hearts Club Band* © Northern Songs, 1967.

"Magical Mystery Tour," words and music by John Lennon and Paul McCartney. Album: *Magical Mystery Tour* © Northern Songs, 1967.

INDEX